RUDYARD KIPLING

VOLUME XXVII

THE YEARS BETWEEN
AND
POEMS FROM HISTORY

Rudyard Kipling

THE WRITINGS IN PROSE AND VERSE OF

RUDYARD KIPLING

THE YEARS BETWEEN

AND

POEMS FROM HISTORY

**Fredonia Books
Amsterdam, The Netherlands**

The Years Between and
Poems from History

by
Rudyard Kipling

ISBN 1-58963-114-5

Copyright © 2001 by Fredonia Books

Reprinted from the 1919 edition

Fredonia Books
Amsterdam, The Netherlands
http://www.fredoniabooks.com

In order to make original editions of historical works available to scholars at an economical price, this facsimile of the original edition of 1919 is reproduced from the best available copy and has been digitally enhanced to improve legibility, but the text remains unaltered to retain historical authenticity.

DEDICATION

TO THE SEVEN WATCHMEN

Seven watchmen sitting in a tower,
   Watching what had come upon mankind,
Showed the Man the Glory and the Power,
   And bade him shape the Kingdom to his mind
"All things on Earth your will shall win you."
   ('Twas so their counsel ran)
"But the Kingdom—the Kingdom is within you,"
   Said the Man's own mind to the Man.
       For time, and some time—
As it was in the bitter years before
   So it shall be in the over-sweetened hour—
That a man's mind is wont to tell him more
   Than Seven Watchmen sitting in a tower.

CONTENTS

	PAGE
AMERICAN WAR, THE	170
BELLS AND QUEEN VICTORIA, THE	175
BENEFACTORS, THE	80
BIG STEAMERS	178
'BROWN BESS'	167
CHOICE, THE	31
'CITY OF BRASS, THE'	124
CIVIL WARS, THE	162
COVENANT, THE	12
CRAFTSMAN, THE	75
DANE-GELD	143
DAWN WIND, THE	152
DEAD KING, THE	83
DEATH-BED, A	88
DECLARATION OF LONDON, THE	7
DUTCH IN THE MEDWAY, THE	164

CONTENTS

	PAGE
EN–DOR	46
EPITAPHS	113
FEMALE OF THE SPECIES, THE	107
'FOR ALL WE HAVE AND ARE'	18
FRANCE	13
FRENCH WARS, THE	173
GEHAZI	91
GETHSEMANE	71
GLORY OF THE GARDEN, THE	183
HOLY WAR, THE	33
HOUSES, THE	36
HYÆNAS, THE	56
IRISH GUARDS, THE	40
JUSTICE	130
KING'S JOB, THE	154
LORD ROBERTS	27
MAKING OF ENGLAND, THE	145
MARY'S SON	67
MESOPOTAMIA	54
MY BOY JACK	51
MY FATHER'S CHAIR	151

CONTENTS

	PAGE
NATIVITY, A	43
NATURAL THEOLOGY	101
NORMAN AND SAXON	146
OLDEST SONG, THE	100
OUTLAWS, THE	23
PILGRIM'S WAY, A	96
PIRATES IN ENGLAND, THE	141
PRO-CONSULS, THE	72
QUESTION, THE	29
RECANTATION, A	48
REEDS OF RUNNYMEDE, THE	149
RIVER'S TALE, THE	135
ROMAN CENTURION SPEAKS, THE	137
ROWERS, THE	3
RUSSIA TO THE PACIFISTS	37
SECRET OF THE MACHINES, THE	180
SONG AT COCK-CROW, A	104
SONG IN STORM, A	20
SONG OF THE LATHES, THE	68
SONS OF MARTHA, THE	63
SPIES' MARCH, THE	58

CONTENTS

	PAGE
THINGS AND THE MAN	77
'TOGETHER'	159
ULSTER	9
VERDICTS, THE	52
VETERANS, THE	6
VIRGINITY, THE	94
WITH DRAKE IN THE TROPICS	157
ZION	25

ILLUSTRATIONS

RUDYARD KIPLING . . . . *Frontispiece*

FACING PAGE

"BEAR WITNESS, EARTH, WE HAVE MADE OUR
    CHOICE
       WITH FREEDOM'S BROTHERHOOD!" . . . 32

"GUNS IN FLANDERS — FLANDERS GUNS!
    (I HAD A MAN THAT WORKED 'EM ONCE!)" 68

THE YEARS BETWEEN

THE ROWERS

1902

(When Germany proposed that England should help her in a naval demonstration to collect debts from Venezuela.)

THE banked oars fell an hundred strong,
    And backed and threshed and ground,
But bitter was the rowers' song
    As they brought the war-boat round.

They had no heart for the rally and roar
    That makes the whale-bath smoke—
When the great blades cleave and hold and leave
    As one on the racing stroke.

They sang:—'What reckoning do you keep,
    And steer her by what star,
If we come unscathed from the Southern deep
    To be wrecked on a Baltic bar?

'Last night you swore our voyage was done,
    But seaward still we go.
And you tell us now of a secret vow
    You have made with an open foe!

THE YEARS BETWEEN

'That we must lie off a lightless coast
    And haul and back and veer,
At the will of the breed that have wronged us most
    For a year and a year and a year!

'There was never a shame in Christendie
    They laid not to our door—
And you say we must take the winter sea
    And sail with them once more?

'Look South! The gale is scarce o'erpast
    That stripped and laid us down,
When we stood forth but they stood fast
    And prayed to see us drown.

'Our dead they mocked are scarcely cold,
    Our wounds are bleeding yet—
And you tell us now that our strength is sold
    To help them press for a debt!

''Neath all the flags of all mankind
    That use upon the seas,
Was there no other fleet to find
    That you strike hands with these?

THE ROWERS

'Of evil times that men can choose
  On evil fate to fall,
What brooding Judgment let you loose
  To pick the worst of all?

'In sight of peace—from the Narrow Seas
  O'er half the world to run—
With a cheated crew, to league anew
  With the Goth and the shameless Hun!

THE VETERANS

(Written for the gathering of survivors of the Indian Mutiny, Albert Hall, 1907.)

To-day, across our fathers' graves,
 The astonished years reveal
The remnant of that desperate host
 Which cleansed our East with steel.

Hail and farewell! We greet you here,
 With tears that none will scorn—
O Keepers of the House of old,
 Or ever we were born!

One service more we dare to ask—
 Pray for us, heroes, pray,
That when Fate lays on us our task
 We do not shame the Day!

THE DECLARATION OF LONDON

June 29, 1911

('On the re-assembling of Parliament after the Coronation, the Government have no intention of allowing their followers to vote according to their convictions on the Declaration of London, but insist on a strictly party vote.'—*Daily Papers*.)

We were all one heart and one race
　When the Abbey trumpets blew.
For a moment's breathing-space
　We had forgotten you.
Now you return to your honoured place
　Panting to shame us anew.

We have walked with the Ages dead—
　With our Past alive and ablaze.
And you bid us pawn our honour for bread,
　This day of all the days!
And you cannot wait till our guests are sped,
　Or last week's wreath decays?

THE YEARS BETWEEN

The light is still in our eyes
  Of Faith and Gentlehood,
Of Service and Sacrifice;
  And it does not match our mood,
To turn so soon to your treacheries
  That starve our land of her food.

Our ears still carry the sound
  Of our once Imperial seas,
Exultant after our King was crowned,
  Beneath the sun and the breeze.
It is too early to have them bound
  Or sold at your decrees.

Wait till the memory goes,
  Wait till the visions fade,
We may betray in time, God knows,
  But we would not have it said,
When you make report to our scornful foes,
  That we kissed as we betrayed!

ULSTER

1912

('Their webs shall not become garments, neither shall they cover themselves with their works: their works are works of iniquity and the act of violence is in their hands.'—*Isaiah* lix. 6.)

THE dark eleventh hour
Draws on and sees us sold
To every evil power
We fought against of old.
Rebellion, rapine, hate,
Oppression, wrong and greed
Are loosed to rule our fate,
By England's act and deed.

The Faith in which we stand,
The laws we made and guard,
Our honour, lives, and land
Are given for reward
To Murder done by night,
To Treason taught by day,
To folly, sloth, and spite,
And we are thrust away.

THE YEARS BETWEEN

The blood our fathers spilt,
Our love, our toils, our pains,
Are counted us for guilt,
And only bind our chains.
Before an Empire's eyes
The traitor claims his price.
What need of further lies?
We are the sacrifice.

We asked no more than leave
To reap where we had sown,
Through good and ill to cleave
To our own flag and throne.
Now England's shot and steel
Beneath that flag must show
How loyal hearts should kneel
To England's oldest foe.

We know the war prepared
On every peaceful home,
We know the hells declared
For such as serve not Rome—

ULSTER

The terror, threats, and dread
In market, hearth, and field—
We know, when all is said,
We perish if we yield.

Believe, we dare not boast,
Believe, we do not fear—
We stand to pay the cost
In all that men hold dear.
What answer from the North?
One Law, one Land, one Throne
If England drive us forth
We shall not fall alone.

THE COVENANT

1914

We thought we ranked above the chance of ill.
  Others might fall, not we, for we were wise—
Merchants in freedom. So, of our free-will
  We let our servants drug our strength with lies.
The pleasure and the poison had its way
  On us as on the meanest, till we learned
That he who lies will steal, who steals will slay.
  Neither God's judgment nor man's heart was
    turned.

Yet there remains His Mercy—to be sought
Through wrath and peril till we cleanse the wrong
By that last right which our forefathers claimed
When their Law failed them and its stewards were
    bought.
This is our cause. God help us, and make strong
Our wills to meet Him later, unashamed!

FRANCE

1913

Broke to every known mischance, lifted over all
By the light sane joy of life, the buckler of the Gaul;
Furious in luxury, merciless in toil,
Terrible with strength that draws from her tireless soil;
Strictest judge of her own worth, gentlest of man's mind,
First to follow Truth and last to leave old Truths behind—
France, beloved of every soul that loves its fellow-kind!

Ere our birth (rememberest thou?) side by side we lay
Fretting in the womb of Rome to begin our fray.
Ere men knew our tongues apart, our one task was known—
Each must mould the other's fate as he wrought his own.
To this end we stirred mankind till all Earth was ours,
Till our world-end strifes begat wayside thrones and powers—

THE YEARS BETWEEN

Puppets that we made or broke to bar the other's path—
Necessary, outpost folk, hirelings of our wrath.
To this end we stormed the seas, tack for tack, and burst
Through the doorways of new worlds, doubtful which was first,
Hand on hilt (rememberest thou?) ready for the blow—
Sure, whatever else we met, we should meet our foe.
Spurred or balked at every stride by the other's strength,
So we rode the ages down and every ocean's length!

Where did you refrain from us or we refrain from you?
Ask the wave that has not watched war between us two!
Others held us for a while, but with weaker charms,
These we quitted at the call for each other's arms.
Eager toward the known delight, equally we strove—
Each the other's mystery, terror, need, and love.
To each other's open court with our proofs we came.

FRANCE

Where could we find honour else, or men to test
  our claim?
From each other's throat we wrenched—valour's
  last reward—
That extorted word of praise gasped 'twixt lunge
  and guard.
In each other's cup we poured mingled blood and
  tears,
Brutal joys, unmeasured hopes, intolerable fears—
All that soiled or salted life for a thousand years.
Proved beyond the need of proof, matched in every
  clime,
O companion, we have lived greatly through all
  time!

Yoked in knowledge and remorse, now we come to
  rest,
Laughing at old villainies that Time has turned to
  jest;
Pardoning old necessities no pardon can efface—
That undying sin we shared in Rouen market-place.
Now we watch the new years shape, wondering if
  they hold

THE YEARS BETWEEN

Fiercer lightnings in their heart than we launched of old.
Now we hear new voices rise, question, boast or gird,
As we raged (rememberest thou?) when our crowds were stirred.
Now we count new keels afloat, and new hosts on land,
Massed like ours (rememberest thou?) when our strokes were planned.
We were schooled for dear life's sake, to know each other's blade.
What can blood and iron make more than we have made?
We have learned by keenest use to know each other's mind.
What shall blood and iron loose that we cannot bind?
We who swept each other's coast, sacked each other's home,
Since the sword of Brennus clashed on the scales at Rome,

FRANCE

Listen, count and close again, wheeling girth to girth,
In the linked and steadfast guard set for peace on earth!

Broke to every known mischance, lifted over all
By the light sane joy of life, the buckler of the Gaul;
Furious in luxury, merciless in toil,
Terrible with strength renewed from a tireless soil;
Strictest judge of her own worth, gentlest of man's mind,
First to face the Truth and last to leave old Truths behind—
France, beloved of every soul that loves or serves its kind!

FOR ALL WE HAVE AND ARE'

1914

For all we have and are,
For all our children's fate,
Stand up and take the war,
The Hun is at the gate!
Our world has passed away,
In wantonness o'erthrown.
There is nothing left to-day
But steel and fire and stone!
    Though all we knew depart,
    The old Commandments stand
    'In courage keep your heart,
    In strength lift up your hand.

Once more we hear the word
That sickened earth of old:—
'No law except the Sword
Unsheathed and uncontrolled.'
Once more it knits mankind,
Once more the nations go
To meet and break and bind
A crazed and driven foe.

'FOR ALL WE HAVE AND ARE'

Comfort, content, delight,
The ages' slow-bought gain,
They shrivelled in a night.
Only ourselves remain
To face the naked days
In silent fortitude,
Through perils and dismays
Renewed and re-renewed.
    Though all we made depart,
    The old Commandments stand:—
    'In patience keep your heart,
    In strength lift up your hand.'

No easy hope or lies
Shall bring us to our goal,
But iron sacrifice
Of body, will, and soul.
There is but one task for all—
One life for each to give.
Who stands if Freedom fall?
Who dies if England live?

A SONG IN STORM

Be well assured that on our side
  The abiding oceans fight,
Though headlong wind and heaping tide
  Make us their sport to-night.
By force of weather not of war
  In jeopardy we steer,
Then welcome Fate's discourtesy
  Whereby it shall appear,
    How in all time of our distress,
    And our deliverance too,
    The game is more than the player of the game,
    And the ship is more than the crew.

Out of the mist into the mirk
  The glimmering combers roll.
Almost these mindless waters work
  As though they had a soul—
Almost as though they leagued to whelm
  Our flag beneath their green:
Then welcome Fate's discourtesy
  Whereby it shall be seen, etc.

A SONG IN STORM

Be well assured, though wave and wind
   Have weightier blows in store,
That we who keep the watch assigned
   Must stand to it the more;
And as our streaming bows rebuke
   Each billow's baulked career,
Sing, welcome Fate's discourtesy
   Whereby it is made clear, etc.

No matter though our deck be swept
   And masts and timber crack—
We can make good all loss except
   The loss of turning back.
So, 'twixt these Devils and our deep
   Let courteous trumpets sound,
To welcome Fate's discourtesy
   Whereby it will be found, etc.

Be well assured, though in our power
   Is nothing left to give
But chance and place to meet the hour,
   And leave to strive to live,

THE YEARS BETWEEN

Till these dissolve our Order holds,
   Our Service binds us here.
Then welcome Fate's discourtesy
   Whereby it is made clear,
     How in all time of our distress,
     And in our triumph too,
      The game is more than the player of the game,
      And the ship is more than the crew!

THE OUTLAWS

1914

Through learned and laborious years
  They set themselves to find
Fresh terrors and undreamed-of fears
  To heap upon mankind.

All that they drew from Heaven above
  Or digged from earth beneath,
They laid into their treasure-trove
  And arsenals of death:

While, for well-weighed advantage sake,
  Ruler and ruled alike
Built up the faith they meant to break
  When the fit hour should strike.

They traded with the careless earth
  And good return it gave;
They plotted by their neighbour's hearth
  The means to make him slave.

THE YEARS BETWEEN

When all was ready to their hand
   They loosed their hidden sword,
And utterly laid waste a land
   Their oath was pledged to guard.

Coldly they went about to raise
   To life and make more dread
Abominations of old days,
   That men believed were dead.

They paid the price to reach their goal
   Across a world in flame;
But their own hate slew their own soul
   Before that victory came.

ZION

The Doorkeepers of Zion,
  They do not always stand
In helmet and whole armour,
  With halberds in their hand;
But, being sure of Zion,
  And all her mysteries,
They rest awhile in Zion,
Sit down and smile in Zion;
Ay, even jest in Zion;
  In Zion, at their ease.

The Gatekeepers of Baal,
  They dare not sit or lean,
But fume and fret and posture
  And foam and curse between;

For being bound to Baal,
  Whose sacrifice is vain,
Their rest is scant with Baal,
They glare and pant for Baal,
They mouth and rant for Baal,
  For Baal in their pain!

THE YEARS BETWEEN

But we will go to Zion,
   By choice and not through dread,
With these our present comrades
   And those our present dead;
And, being free of Zion
   In both her fellowships,
Sit down and sup in Zion—
Stand up and drink in Zion
Whatever cup in Zion
   Is offered to our lips!

LORD ROBERTS
1914

He passed in the very battle-smoke
  Of the war that he had descried.
Three hundred mile of cannon spoke
  When the Master-Gunner died.

He passed to the very sound of the guns;
  But, before his eye grew dim,
He had seen the faces of the sons
  Whose sires had served with him.

He had touched their sword-hilts and greeted each
  With the old sure word of praise;
And there was virtue in touch and speech
  As it had been in old days.

So he dismissed them and took his rest,
  And the steadfast spirit went forth
Between the adoring East and West
  And the tireless guns of the North.

THE YEARS BETWEEN

Clean, simple, valiant, well-beloved,
  Flawless in faith and fame,
Whom neither ease nor honours moved
  An hair's-breadth from his aim.

Never again the war-wise face,
  The weighed and urgent word
That pleaded in the market-place—
  Pleaded and was not heard!

Yet from his life a new life springs
  Through all the hosts to come,
And Glory is the least of things
  That follow this man home.

THE QUESTION
1916

BRETHREN, how shall it fare with me
　When the war is laid aside,
If it be proven that I am he
　For whom a world has died?

If it be proven that all my good,
　And the greater good I will make,
Were purchased me by a multitude
　Who suffered for my sake?

That I was delivered by mere mankind
　Vowed to one sacrifice,
And not, as I hold them, battle-blind,
　But dying with open eyes?

That they did not ask me to draw the sword
　When they stood to endure their lot—
That they only looked to me for a word,
　And I answered I knew them not?

THE YEARS BETWEEN

If it be found, when the battle clears,
    Their death has set me free,
Then how shall I live with myself through the years
    Which they have bought for me?

Brethren, how must it fare with me,
    Or how am I justified,
If it be proven that I am he
    For whom mankind has died;
If it be proven that I am he
    Who being questioned denied?

THE CHOICE
1917

(THE AMERICAN SPIRIT SPEAKS)

To the Judge of Right and Wrong
  With Whom fulfilment lies
Our purpose and our power belong,
  Our faith and sacrifice.

Let Freedom's Land rejoice!
  Our ancient bonds are riven;
Once more to us the eternal choice
  Of Good or Ill is given.

Not at a little cost,
  Hardly by prayer or tears,
Shall we recover the road we lost
  In the drugged and doubting years

But, after the fires and the wrath,
  But, after searching and pain,
His Mercy opens us a path
  To live with ourselves again.

THE YEARS BETWEEN

In the Gates of Death rejoice!
  We see and hold the good—
Bear witness, Earth, we have made our choice
  With Freedom's brotherhood!

Then praise the Lord Most High
  Whose Strength hath saved us whole,
Who bade us choose that the Flesh should die
  And not the living Soul!

To the God in Man displayed—
  Where e'er we see that Birth,
Be love and understanding paid
  As never yet on earth!

To the Spirit that moves in Man,
  On Whom all worlds depend,
Be Glory since our world began
  And service to the end!

THE HOLY WAR

1917

('For here lay the excellent wisdom of him that built Mansoul, that the walls could never be broken down nor hurt by the most mighty adverse potentate unless the townsmen gave consent thereto.'
—BUNYAN'S *Holy War*.)

A TINKER *out of Bedford,*
  A vagrant oft in quod,
A private under Fairfax,
  A minister of God—
Two hundred years and thirty
  Ere Armageddon came
His single hand portrayed it,
  And Bunyan was his name!

He mapped, for those who follow,
  The world in which we are—
'This famous town of Mansoul'
  That takes the Holy War.
Her true and traitor people,
  The gates along her wall,
From Eye Gate unto Feel Gate,
  John Bunyan showed them all.

THE YEARS BETWEEN

All enemy divisions,
  Recruits of every class,
And highly-screened positions
  For flame or poison-gas;
The craft that we call modern,
  The crimes that we call new,
John Bunyan had 'em typed and filed
  In Sixteen Eighty-two.

Likewise the Lords of Looseness
  That hamper faith and works,
The Perseverance-Doubters,
  And Present-Comfort shirks,
With brittle intellectuals
  Who crack beneath a strain—
John Bunyan met that helpful set
  In Charles the Second's reign.

Emmanuel's vanguard dying
  For right and not for rights,

THE HOLY WAR

My Lord Apollyon lying
  To the State-kept Stockholmites,
The Pope, the swithering Neutrals,
  The Kaiser and his Gott—
Their rôles, their goals, their naked souls
  He knew and drew the lot.

Now he hath left his quarters,
  In Bunhill Fields to lie,
The wisdom that he taught us
  Is proven prophecy—
One watchword through our armies,
  One answer from our lands:—
'No dealings with Diabolus
  As long as Mansoul stands!'

A pedlar from a hovel,
  The lowest of the low,
The father of the Novel,
  Salvation's first Defoe,
Eight blinded generations
  Ere Armageddon came,
He showed us how to meet it,
  And Bunyan was his name!

THE HOUSES

(A SONG OF THE DOMINIONS)

1898

'TWIXT my house and thy house the pathway is broad,
In thy house or my house is half the world's hoard;
By my house and thy house hangs all the world's fate,
On thy house and my house lies half the world's hate.

For my house and thy house no help shall we find
Save thy house and my house—kin cleaving to kind:
If my house be taken, thine tumbleth anon,
If thy house be forfeit, mine followeth soon.

'Twixt my house and thy house what talk can there be
Of headship or lordship, of service or fee?
Since my house to thy house no greater can send
Than thy house to my house—friend comforting friend;
And thy house to my house no meaner can bring
Than my house to thy house—King counselling King.

RUSSIA TO THE PACIFISTS

God rest you, peaceful gentlemen, let nothing you dismay,
But—leave your sports a little while—the dead are borne this way!
Armies dead and Cities dead, past all count or care.
God rest you, merry gentlemen, what portent see you there?
    Singing:—Break ground for a wearied host
        That have no ground to keep.
        Give them the rest that they covet most . . .
        And who shall next to sleep, good sirs,
        In such a trench to sleep?

God rest you, peaceful gentlemen, but give us leave to pass.
We go to dig a nation's grave as great as England was.
For this Kingdom and this Glory and this Power and this Pride

THE YEARS BETWEEN

Three hundred years it flourished—in three hundred
   days it died.
     Singing:—Pour oil for a frozen throng,
       That lie about the ways.
       Give them the warmth they have lacked
          so long . . .
       And what shall be next to blaze, good
          sirs,
       On such a pyre to blaze?

God rest you, thoughtful gentlemen, and send your
   sleep is light!
Remains of this dominion no shadow, sound, or
   sight,
Except the sound of weeping and the sight of burn-
   ing fire,
And the shadow of a people that is trampled into
   mire.
     Singing:—Break bread for a starving folk
       That perish in the field.
       Give them their food as they take the
          yoke . . .
       And who shall be next to yield, good sirs,
       For such a bribe to yield?

RUSSIA TO THE PACIFISTS

God rest you, merry gentlemen, and keep you in your mirth!
Was ever kingdom turned so soon to ashes, blood, and earth?
'Twixt the summer and the snow—seeding-time and frost—
Arms and victual, hope and counsel, name and country lost!
> Singing:—*Let down by the foot and the head—*
> *Shovel and smooth it all!*
> *So do we bury a Nation dead . . .*
> And who shall be next to fall, good sirs,
> With your good help to fall?

THE IRISH GUARDS

1918

WE'RE not so old in the Army List,
   But we're not so young at our trade,
For we had the honour at Fontenoy
   Of meeting the Guards' Brigade.
'Twas Lally, Dillon, Bulkeley, Clare,
   And Lee that led us then,
And after a hundred and seventy years
   We're fighting for France again!
     Old Days! The wild geese are flighting,
       Head to the storm as they faced it before!
       For where there are Irish there's bound to be fighting,
       And when there's no fighting, it's Ireland no more!
                   Ireland no more!

The fashion's all for khaki now,
   But once through France we went
Full-dressed in scarlet Army cloth,
   The English—left at Ghent.
They're fighting on our side to-day
   But, before they changed their clothes,

THE IRISH GUARDS

The half of Europe knew our fame,
  As all of Ireland knows!
    Old Days! The wild geese are flying,
      Head to the storm as they faced it before!
    For where there are Irish there's memory undying,
      And when we forget, it is Ireland no more!
                    Ireland no more!

From Barry Wood to Gouzeaucourt,
  From Boyne to Pilkem Ridge,
The ancient days come back no more
  Than water under the bridge.
But the bridge it stands and the water runs
  As red as yesterday,
And the Irish move to the sound of the guns
  Like salmon to the sea.
    Old Days! The wild geese are ranging,
      Head to the storm as they faced it before!
    For where there are Irish their hearts are unchanging,
      And when they are changed, it is Ireland no more!
                    Ireland no more!

THE YEARS BETWEEN

We're not so old in the Army List,
  But we're not so new in the ring,
For we carried our packs with Marshal Saxe
  When Louis was our King.
But Douglas Haig's our Marshal now,
  And we're King George's men,
And after one hundred and seventy years
  We're fighting for France again!
> *Ah, France! And did we stand by you,*
>   *When life was made splendid with gifts and rewards?*
> *Ah, France! And will we deny you*
>   *In the hour of your agony, Mother of Swords?*
> *Old Days! The wild geese are flighting,*
>   *Head to the storm as they faced it before!*
> *For where there are Irish there's loving and fighting,*
>   *And when we stop either, it's Ireland no more!*
>   *Ireland no more!*

A NATIVITY

1916

The Babe was laid in the Manger
  Between the gentle kine—
All safe from cold and danger—
  'But it was not so with mine.
            (With mine! With mine!)
Is it well with the child, is it well?'
  The waiting mother prayed.
'For I know not how he fell,
  And I know not where he is laid.'

A Star stood forth in Heaven;
  The watchers ran to see
The Sign of the Promise given—
  'But there comes no sign to me.
            (To me! To me!)
'*My* child died in the dark.
  Is it well with the child, is it well?
There was none to tend him or mark,
  And I know not how he fell.'

THE YEARS BETWEEN

The Cross was raised on high;
  The Mother grieved beside—
'But the Mother saw Him die
  And took Him when He died.
                (He died! He died!)
'Seemly and undefiled
  His burial-place was made—
Is it well, is it well with the child?
  For I know not where he is laid.'

On the dawning of Easter Day
  Comes Mary Magdalene;
But the Stone was rolled away,
  And the Body was not within—
                (Within! Within!)
'Ah, who will answer my word?'
  The broken mother prayed.
'They have taken away my Lord,
  And I know not where He is laid.'

. . . .

A NATIVITY

The Star stands forth in Heaven.
  The watchers watch in vain
For a Sign of the Promise given
  Of peace on Earth again—
                    (Again! Again!)
'But I know for Whom he fell'—
  The steadfast mother smiled.
'Is it well with the child—is it well?
  It is well—it is well with the child!'

EN-DOR

('Behold there is a woman that hath a familiar spirit at En-dor.'—
1 *Samuel* xxviii. 7.)

THE road to En-dor is easy to tread
  For Mother or yearning Wife.
There, it is sure, we shall meet our Dead
  As they were even in life.
Earth has not dreamed of the blessing in store
For desolate hearts on the road to En-dor.

Whispers shall comfort us out of the dark—
  Hands—ah God!—that we knew!
Visions and voices—look and heark!—
  Shall prove that our tale is true,
And that those who have passed to the further shore
May be hailed—at a price—on the road to En-dor.

But they are so deep in their new eclipse
  Nothing they say can reach,
Unless it be uttered by alien lips
  And framed in a stranger's speech.
The son must send word to the mother that bore,
Through an hireling's mouth. 'Tis the rule of En-dor.

EN-DOR

And not for nothing these gifts are shown
  By such as delight our dead.
They must twitch and stiffen and slaver and groan
  Ere the eyes are set in the head,
And the voice from the belly begins. Therefore,
We pay them a wage where they ply at En-dor.

Even so, we have need of faith
  And patience to follow the clue.
Often, at first, what the dear one saith
  Is babble, or jest, or untrue.
(Lying spirits perplex us sore
Till our loves—and our lives—are well-known at
    En-dor). . . .

Oh the road to En-dor is the oldest road
  And the craziest road of all!
Straight it runs to the Witch's abode,
  As it did in the days of Saul,
And nothing has changed of the sorrow in store
For such as go down on the road to En-dor!

A RECANTATION

(TO LYDE OF THE MUSIC HALLS)

What boots it on the Gods to call?
  Since, answered or unheard,
We perish with the Gods and all
  Things made—except the Word.

Ere certain Fate had touched a heart
  By fifty years made cold,
I judged thee, Lyde, and thy art
  O'erblown and over-bold.

But he—but he, of whom bereft
  I suffer vacant days—
He on his shield not meanly left—
  He cherished all thy lays.

Witness the magic coffer stocked
  With convoluted runes
Wherein thy very voice was locked
  And linked to circling tunes.

A RECANTATION

Witness thy portrait, smoke-defiled,
    That decked his shelter-place.
Life seemed more present, wrote the child,
    Beneath thy well-known face.

And when the grudging days restored
    Him for a breath to home,
He, with fresh crowds of youth, adored
    Thee making mirth in Rome.

Therefore, I, humble, join the hosts,
    Loyal and loud, who bow
To thee as Queen of Songs—and ghosts—
    For I remember how

Never more rampant rose the Hall
    At thy audacious line
Than when the news came in from Gaul
    Thy son had—followed mine.

But thou didst hide it in thy breast
    And, capering, took the brunt
Of blaze and blare, and launched the jest
    That swept next week the front.

THE YEARS BETWEEN

Singer to children! Ours possessed
  Sleep before noon—but thee,
Wakeful each midnight for the rest,
  No holocaust shall free.

Yet they who use the Word assigned,
  To hearten and make whole,
Not less than Gods have served mankind,
  Though vultures rend their soul.

MY BOY JACK

'Have you news of my boy Jack?'
  Not this tide.
'When d'you think that he'll come back?'
  Not with this wind blowing, and this tide.

'Has any one else had word of him?'
  Not this tide.
For what is sunk will hardly swim,
  Not with this wind blowing, and this tide.

'Oh, dear, what comfort can I find?'
  None this tide,
  Nor any tide,
Except he did not shame his kind—
  Not even with that wind blowing, and that tide

Then hold your head up all the more,
  This tide,
  And every tide;
Because he was the son you bore,
  And gave to that wind blowing and that tide!

THE VERDICTS

(JUTLAND)

Not in the thick of the fight,
  Not in the press of the odds,
Do the heroes come to their height,
  Or we know the demi-gods.

That stands over till peace.
  We can only perceive
Men returned from the seas,
  Very grateful for leave.

They grant us sudden days
  Snatched from their business of war;
But we are too close to appraise
  What manner of men they are.

And, whether their names go down
  With age-kept victories,
Or whether they battle and drown
  Unreckoned, is hid from our eyes.

THE VERDICTS

They are too near to be great,
  But our children shall understand
When and how our fate
  Was changed, and by whose hand.

Our children shall measure their worth.
  We are content to be blind . . .
But we know that we walk on a new-born earth
  With the saviours of mankind.

MESOPOTAMIA
1917

They shall not return to us, the resolute, the young,
    The eager and whole-hearted whom we gave:
But the men who left them thriftily to die in their own dung,
    Shall they come with years and honour to the grave?

They shall not return to us, the strong men coldly slain
    In sight of help denied from day to day:
But the men who edged their agonies and chid them in their pain,
    Are they too strong and wise to put away?

Our dead shall not return to us while Day and Night divide—
    Never while the bars of sunset hold:
But the idle-minded overlings who quibbled while they died,
    Shall they thrust for high employments as of old?

MESOPOTAMIA

Shall we only threaten and be angry for an hour?
 When the storm is ended shall we find
How softly but how swiftly they have sidled back
 to power
 By the favour and contrivance of their kind?

Even while they soothe us, while they promise large
 amends,
 Even while they make a show of fear,
Do they call upon their debtors, and take council
 with their friends,
 To confirm and re-establish each career?

Their lives cannot repay us—their death could not
 undo—
 The shame that they have laid upon our race:
But the slothfulness that wasted and the arrogance
 that slew,
 Shall we leave it unabated in its place?

THE HYÆNAS

AFTER the burial-parties leave
    And the baffled kites have fled;
The wise hyænas come out at eve
    To take account of our dead.

How he died and why he died
    Troubles them not a whit.
They snout the bushes and stones aside
    And dig till they come to it.

They are only resolute they shall eat
    That they and their mates may thrive,
And they know that the dead are safer meat
    Than the weakest thing alive.

(For a goat may butt, and a worm may sting,
    And a child will sometimes stand;
But a poor dead soldier of the King
    Can never lift a hand.)

THE HYÆNAS

They whoop and halloo and scatter the dirt
  Until their tushes white
Take good hold in the army shirt,
  And tug the corpse to light.

And the pitiful face is shewn again
  For an instant ere they close;
But it is not discovered to living men—
  Only to God and to those

Who, being soulless, are free from shame,
  Whatever meat they may find.
Nor do they defile the dead man's name—
  That is reserved for his kind.

THE SPIES' MARCH

(BEFORE THE WAR)

('The outbreak is in full swing and our death-rate would sicken Napoleon. . . . Dr. M—— died last week, and C—— on Monday, but some more medicines are coming. . . . We don't seem to be able to check it at all. . . . Villages panicking badly. . . . In some places not a living soul. . . . But at any rate the experience gained may come in useful, so I am keeping my notes written up to date in case of accidents. . . . Death is a queer chap to live with for steady company.'—*Extract from a private letter from Manchuria.*)

THERE are no leaders to lead us to honour, and yet
    without leaders we sally,
Each man reporting for duty alone, out of sight,
    out of reach, of his fellow.
There are no bugles to call the battalions, and yet
    without bugles we rally
From the ends of the earth to the ends of the earth,
    to follow the Standard of Yellow!
    Fall in! O fall in! O fall in!

THE SPIES' MARCH

Not where the squadrons mass,
   Not where the bayonets shine,
Not where the big shell shout as they pass
   Over the firing-line;
Not where the wounded are,
   Not where the nations die,
Killed in the cleanly game of war—
   That is no place for a spy!
O Princes, Thrones and Powers, your work
     is less than ours—
   Here is no place for a spy!

Trained to another use,
   We march with colours furled,
Only concerned when Death breaks loose
   On a front of half a world.
Only for General Death
   The Yellow Flag may fly,
While we take post beneath—
   That is the place for a spy.
Where Plague has spread his pinions over
     Nations and Dominions—
   Then will be work for a spy!

THE YEARS BETWEEN

The dropping shots begin,
  The single funerals pass,
Our skirmishers run in,
  The corpses dot the grass!
The howling towns stampede,
  The tainted hamlets die.
Now it is war indeed—
  Now there is room for a spy!
O Peoples, Kings and Lands, we are waiting
    your commands—
  What is the work for a spy?
      (DRUMS)—*Fear is upon us, spy!*

'Go where his pickets hide—
  Unmask the shapes they take,
Whether a gnat from the waterside,
  Or stinging fly in the brake,
Or filth of the crowded street,
  Or a sick rat limping by,
Or a smear of spittle dried in the heat—
  That is the work of a spy!
      (DRUMS)—*Death is upon us, spy!*

THE SPIES' MARCH

'What does he next prepare?
  Whence will he move to attack?—
By water, earth or air?—
  How can we head him back?
Shall we starve him out if we burn
  Or bury his food-supply?
Slip through his lines and learn—
  That is work for a spy!
    (DRUMS)—*Get to your business, spy!*

'Does he feint or strike in force?
  Will he charge or ambuscade?
What is it checks his course?
  Is he beaten or only delayed?
How long will the lull endure?
  Is he retreating? Why?
Crawl to his camp and make sure—
  That is the work for a spy!
    (DRUMS)—*Fetch us our answer, spy!*

THE YEARS BETWEEN

'Ride with him girth to girth
  Wherever the Pale Horse wheels,
Wait on his councils, ear to earth,
  And say what the dust reveals.
For the smoke of our torment rolls
  Where the burning thousands lie;
What do we care for men's bodies or souls?
  Bring us deliverance, spy!'

THE SONS OF MARTHA

The Sons of Mary seldom bother, for they have
    inherited that good part;
But the Sons of Martha favour their Mother of the
    careful soul and the troubled heart.
And because she lost her temper once, and because
    she was rude to the Lord her Guest,
Her Sons must wait upon Mary's Sons, world with-
    out end, reprieve, or rest.

It is their care in all the ages to take the buffet
    and cushion the shock.
It is their care that the gear engages; it is their
    care that the switches lock.
It is their care that the wheels run truly; it is their
    care to embark and entrain,
Tally, transport, and deliver duly the Sons of Mary
    by land and main.

THE YEARS BETWEEN

They say to mountains, 'Be ye removèd.' They
  say to the lesser floods 'Be dry.'
Under their rods are the rocks reprovèd—they are
  not afraid of that which is high.
Then do the hill-tops shake to the summit—then
  is the bed of the deep laid bare,
That the Sons of Mary may overcome it, pleasantly
  sleeping and unaware.

They finger death at their gloves' end where they
  piece and repiece the living wires.
He rears against the gates they tend: they feed him
  hungry behind their fires.
Early at dawn, ere men see clear, they stumble into
  his terrible stall,
And hale him forth like a haltered steer, and goad
  and turn him till evenfall.

THE SONS OF MARTHA

To these from birth is Belief forbidden; from these till death is Relief afar.
They are concerned with matters hidden—under the earth-line their altars are:
The secret fountains to follow up, waters withdrawn to restore to the mouth,
And gather the floods as in a cup, and pour them again at a city's drouth.

They do not preach that their God will rouse them a little before the nuts work loose.
They do not teach that His Pity allows them to leave their work when they damn-well choose.
As in the thronged and the lighted ways, so in the dark and the desert they stand,
Wary and watchful all their days that their brethren's days may be long in the land.

THE YEARS BETWEEN

Raise ye the stone or cleave the wood to make a path more fair or flat;
Lo, it is black already with blood some Son of Martha spilled for that!
Not as a ladder from earth to Heaven, not as a witness to any creed,
But simple service simply given to his own kind in their common need.

And the Sons of Mary smile and are blessèd—they know the angels are on their side.
They know in them is the Grace confessèd, and for them are the Mercies multiplied.
They sit at the Feet—they hear the Word—they see how truly the Promise runs:
They have cast their burden upon the Lord, and—the Lord He lays it on Martha's Sons!

MARY'S SON

I F you stop to find out what your wages will be
   And how they will clothe and feed you,
Willie, my son, don't you go on the Sea,
   For the Sea will never need you.

If you ask for the reason of every command,
   And argue with people about you,
Willie, my son, don't you go on the Land,
   For the Land will do better without you.

If you stop to consider the work you have done
   And to boast what your labour is worth, dear,
Angels may come for you, Willie, my son,
   But you'll never be wanted on Earth, dear!

THE SONG OF THE LATHES
1918

(Being the words of the tune hummed at her lathe by Mrs. L. Embsay, widow.)

THE fans and the beltings they roar round me.
The power is shaking the floor round me
Till the lathes pick up their duty and the midnight-shift takes over.
> It is good for me to be here!

Guns in Flanders—Flanders guns!
(I had a man that worked 'em once!)
Shells for guns in Flanders, Flanders!
Shells for guns in Flanders, Flanders!
> *Shells for guns in Flanders! Feed the guns!*

The cranes and the carriers they boom over me,
The bays and the galleries they loom over me,
With their quarter-mile of pillars growing little in the distance:
> It is good for me to be here!

THE SONG OF THE LATHES

The Zeppelins and Gothas they raid over us.
Our lights give warning, and fade over us.
(Seven thousand women keeping quiet in the darkness!)
    Oh, it is good for me to be here!

The roofs and the buildings they grow round me,
Eating up the fields I used to know round me;
And the shed that I began in is a sub-inspector's office—
    So long have I been here!

I've seen six hundred mornings make our lamps grow dim,
Through the bit that isn't painted round our skylight rim,
And the sunshine in the window slope according to the seasons,
    Twice since I've been here.

THE YEARS BETWEEN

The trains on the sidings they call to us
With the hundred thousand blanks that they
    haul to us;
And we send 'em what we've finished, and they
    take it where it's wanted,
        For that is why we are here!

Man's hate passes as his love will pass.
God made woman what she always was.
Them that bear the burden they will never grant
    forgiveness
        So long as they are here!

Once I was a woman, but that's by with me.
All I loved and looked for, it must die with me.
But the Lord has left me over for a servant of the
    Judgment,
        And I serve His Judgments here!

Guns in Flanders—Flanders guns!
(I had a son that worked 'em once!)
Shells for guns in Flanders, Flanders!
Shells for guns in Flanders, Flanders!
        Shells for guns in Flanders! Feed the guns!

GETHSEMANE

The Garden called Gethsemane
  In Picardy it was,
And there the people came to see
  The English soldiers pass.
We used to pass—we used to pass
  Or halt, as it might be,
And ship our masks in case of gas
  Beyond Gethsemane.

The Garden called Gethsemane,
  It held a pretty lass,
But all the time she talked to me
  I prayed my cup might pass.
The officer sat on the chair,
  The men lay on the grass,
And all the time we halted there
  I prayed my cup might pass—

It didn't pass—it didn't pass—
  It didn't pass from me.
I drank it when we met the gas
  Beyond Gethsemane.

THE PRO-CONSULS

The overfaithful sword returns the user
His heart's desire at price of his heart's blood.
The clamour of the arrogant accuser
Wastes that one hour we needed to make good.
This was foretold of old at our outgoing;
This we accepted who have squandered, knowing,
The strength and glory of our reputations,
At the day's need, as it were dross, to guard
The tender and new-dedicate foundations
Against the sea we fear—not man's award.

They that dig foundations deep,
   Fit for realms to rise upon,
Little honour do they reap
   Of their generation,
Any more than mountains gain
Stature till we reach the plain.

With no veil before their face
   Such as shroud or sceptre lend—
Daily in the market-place,
   Of one height to foe and friend—

THE PRO-CONSULS

They must cheapen self to find
Ends uncheapened for mankind.

Through the night when hirelings rest,
   Sleepless they arise, alone,
The unsleeping arch to test
   And the o'er-trusted corner-stone,
'Gainst the need, they know, that lies
Hid behind the centuries.

Not by lust of praise or show
   Not by Peace herself betrayed—
Peace herself must they forego
   Till that peace be fitly made;
And in single strength uphold
Wearier hands and hearts acold.

On the stage their act hath framed
   For thy sports, O Liberty!
Doubted are they, and defamed
   By the tongues their act set free,
While they quicken, tend and raise
Power that must their power displace.

THE YEARS BETWEEN

Lesser men feign greater goals,
   Failing whereof they may sit
Scholarly to judge the souls
   That go down into the pit,
And, despite its certain clay,
Heave a new world towards the day.

These at labour make no sign,
   More than planets, tides or years
Which discover God's design,
   Not our hopes and not our fears;
Nor in aught they gain or lose
Seek a triumph or excuse.

For, so the Ark be borne to Zion, who
Heeds how they perished or were paid that bore it?
For, so the Shrine abide, what shame—what pride—
If we, the priests, were bound or crowned before it?

THE CRAFTSMAN

Once, after long-drawn revel at The Mermaid,
He to the overbearing Boanerges
Jonson, uttered (If half of it were liquor,
        Blessed be the vintage!)

Saying how, at an alehouse under Cotswold,
He had made sure of his very Cleopatra,
Drunk with enormous, salvation-contemning
        Love for a tinker.

How, while he hid from Sir Thomas's keepers,
Crouched in a ditch and drenched by the midnight
Dews, he had listened to gipsy Juliet
        Rail at the dawning.

How at Bankside, a boy drowning kittens
Winced at the business; whereupon his sister
(Lady Macbeth aged seven) thrust 'em under,
        Sombrely scornful.

THE YEARS BETWEEN

How on a Sabbath, hushed and compassionate—
She being known since her birth to the townsfolk
Stratford dredged and delivered from Avon
                Dripping Ophelia.

So, with a thin third finger marrying
Drop to wine-drop domed on the table,
Shakespeare opened his heart till sunrise
                Entered to hear him.

London wakened and he, imperturbable,
Passed from waking to hurry after shadows . . .
Busied upon shows of no earthly importance?
                Yes, but he knew it!

THINGS AND THE MAN

(IN MEMORIAM, JOSEPH CHAMBERLAIN)

1904

'And Joseph dreamed a dream, and he told it his brethren and they hated him yet the more.'—*Genesis* xxxvii. 5.

Oh ye who hold the written clue
  To all save all unwritten things,
And, half a league behind, pursue
  The accomplished Fact with flouts and flings,
  Look! To your knee your baby brings
    The oldest tale since Earth began—
The answer to your worryings:
    '*Once on a time there was a Man.*'

He, single-handed, met and slew
  Magicians, Armies, Ogres, Kings.
He lonely 'mid his doubting crew—
  'In all the loneliness of wings'—

THE YEARS BETWEEN

He fed the flame, he filled the springs,
   He locked the ranks, he launched the van
Straight at the grinning Teeth of Things.
   'Once on a time there was a Man.'

The peace of shocked Foundations flew
   Before his ribald questionings.
He broke the Oracles in two,
   And bared the paltry wires and strings.
He headed desert wanderings;
   He led his soul, his cause, his clan
A little from the ruck of Things.
   'Once on a time there was a Man.'

Thrones, Powers, Dominions block the view
   With episodes and underlings—
The meek historian deems them true
   Nor heeds the song that Clio sings—
   The simple central truth that stings
   The mob to boo, the priest to ban;
Things never yet created things—
   'Once on a time there was a Man.'

THINGS AND THE MAN

A bolt is fallen from the blue.
  A wakened realm full circle swings
Where Dothan's dreamer dreams anew
  Of vast and farborne harvestings;
  And unto him an Empire clings
    That grips the purpose of his plan.
  My Lords, how think you of these things?
    Once—in our time—is there a Man?

THE BENEFACTORS

*A*H *! What avails the classic bent*
  And what the cultured word,
Against the undoctored incident
  That actually occurred?

And what is Art whereto we press
  Through paint and prose and rhyme
When Nature in her nakedness
  Defeats us every time?

It is not learning, grace nor gear,
  Nor easy meat and drink,
But bitter pinch of pain and fear
  That makes creation think.

When in this world's unpleasing youth
  Our god-like race began,
The longest arm, the sharpest tooth,
  Gave man control of man;

THE BENEFACTORS

Till, bruised and bitten to the bone
    And taught by pain and fear,
He learned to deal the far-off stone,
    And poke the long, safe spear.

So tooth and nail were obsolete
    As means against a foe,
Till, bored by uniform defeat,
    Some genius built the bow.

Then stone and javelin proved as vain
    As old-time tooth and nail;
Ere, spurred anew by fear and pain,
    Man fashioned coats of mail.

Then was there safety for the rich
    And danger for the poor,
Till someone mixed a powder which
    Redressed the scale once more.

Helmet and armour disappeared
    With sword and bow and pike,
And, when the smoke of battle cleared,
    All men were armed alike. . . .

THE YEARS BETWEEN

And when ten million such were slain
   To please one crazy king,
Man, schooled in bulk by fear and pain,
   Grew weary of the thing;

And, at the very hour designed,
   To enslave him past recall,
His tooth-stone-arrow-gun-shy mind
   Turned and abolished all.

    .   .   .   .   .

All Power, each Tyrant, every Mob
   Whose head has grown too large,
Ends by destroying its own job
   And earns its own discharge.

And Man, whose mere necessities
   Move all things from his path,
Trembles meanwhile at their decrees,
   And deprecates their wrath!

THE DEAD KING

(EDWARD VII.)

1910

*Who in the Realm to-day lays down dear life for the
  sake of a land more dear?
And, unconcerned for his own estate, toils till the
  last grudged sands have run?
    Let him approach. It is proven here
Our King asks nothing of any man more than Our
  King himself has done.*

For to him above all was Life good, above all he
    commanded
        Her abundance full-handed.
The peculiar treasure of Kings was his for the taking:
All that men come to in dreams he inherited waking:—
His marvel of world-gathered armies—one heart
    and all races;
His seas 'neath his keels when his war-castles foamed
    to their places;

THE YEARS BETWEEN

The thundering foreshores that answered his heralded landing;
The huge lighted cities adoring, the assemblies upstanding;
The Councils of Kings called in haste to learn how he was minded—
The Kingdoms, the Powers, and the Glories he dealt with unblinded.

To him came all captains of men, all achievers of glory,
Hot from the press of their battles they told him their story.
They revealed him their life in an hour and, saluting, departed,
Joyful to labour afresh—he had made them new-hearted.
And, since he weighed men from his youth, and no lie long deceived him,
He spoke and exacted the truth, and the basest believed him.

THE DEAD KING

And God poured him an exquisite wine, that was
    daily renewed to him,
In the clear-welling love of his peoples that daily
    accrued to him.
Honour and service we gave him, rejoicingly fear-
    less;
Faith absolute, trust beyond speech and a friendship
    as peerless.
And since he was Master and Servant in all that
    we asked him,
We leaned hard on his wisdom in all things, know-
    ing not how we tasked him.

For on him each new day laid command, every
    tyrannous hour,
To confront, or confirm, or make smooth some dread
    issue of power;
To deliver true judgment aright at the instant,
    unaided,
In the strict, level, ultimate phrase that allowed or
    dissuaded;

THE YEARS BETWEEN

To foresee, to allay, to avert from us perils unnumbered,
To stand guard on our gates when he guessed that the watchmen had slumbered;
To win time, to turn hate, to woo folly to service and, mightily schooling
His strength to the use of his Nations, to rule as not ruling.
These were the works of our King; Earth's peace was the proof of them.
God gave him great works to fulfil, and to us the behoof of them.
We accepted his toil as our right—none spared, none excused him.
When he was bowed by his burden his rest was refused him.
We troubled his age with our weakness—the blacker our shame to us!
Hearing his People had need of him, straightway he came to us.

THE DEAD KING

As he received so he gave—nothing grudged, naught denying,
Not even the last gasp of his breath when he strove for us, dying.
For our sakes, without question, he put from him all that he cherished.
Simply as any that serve him he served and he perished.
All that Kings covet was his, and he flung it aside for us.
Simply as any that die in his service he died for us.

Who in the Realm to-day has choice of the easy road or the hard to tread?
  And, much concerned for his own estate, would sell his soul to remain in the sun?
    Let him depart nor look on Our dead.
Our King asks nothing of any man more than Our King himself has done.

A DEATH-BED

'THIS is the State above the Law.
   The State exists for the State alone.'
[*This is a gland at the back of the jaw,*
   And an answering lump by the collar-bone.]

Some die shouting in gas or fire;
   Some die silent, by shell and shot.
Some die desperate, caught on the wire;
   Some die suddenly. This will not.

'Regis suprema Voluntas lex'
   [*It will follow the regular course of—throats.*]
Some die pinned by the broken decks,
   Some die sobbing between the boats.

Some die eloquent, pressed to death
   By the sliding trench, as their friends can hear
Some die wholly in half a breath.
   Some—give trouble for half a year.

A DEATH-BED

'There is neither Evil nor Good in life
  Except as the needs of the State ordain.
[*Since it is rather too late for the knife,*
  All we can do is to mask the pain.]

Some die saintly in faith and hope—
  One died thus in a prison-yard—
Some die broken by rape or the rope;
  Some die easily. This dies hard.

'I will dash to pieces who bar my way.
  Woe to the traitor! Woe to the weak!'
[*Let him write what he wishes to say.*
  It tires him out if he tries to speak.]

Some die quietly. Some abound
  In loud self-pity. Others spread
Bad morale through the cots around . . .
  This is a type that is better dead.

'The war was forced on me by my foes.
  All that I sought was the right to live.'
[*Don't be afraid of a triple dose;*
  The pain will neutralize half we give.

THE YEARS BETWEEN

Here are the needles. See that he dies
  While the effects of the drug endure. . . .
What is the question he asks with his eyes?
  Yes, All-Highest, to God, be sure.]

GEHAZI

'Whence comest thou, Gehazi,
  So reverend to behold,
In scarlet and in ermines
  And chain of England's gold?'
'From following after Naaman
  To tell him all is well,
Whereby my zeal hath made me
  A Judge in Israel.'

Well done, well done, Gehazi,
  Stretch forth thy ready hand,
Thou barely 'scaped from judgment,
  Take oath to judge the land,
Unswayed by gift of money
  Or privy bribe, more base,
Of knowledge which is profit
  In any market-place.

THE YEARS BETWEEN

Search out and probe, Gehazi,
  As thou of all canst try,
The truthful, well-weighed answer
  That tells the blacker lie—
The loud, uneasy virtue
  The anger feigned at will,
To overbear a witness
  And make the Court keep still.

Take order now, Gehazi,
  That no man talk aside
In secret with his judges
  The while his case is tried.
Lest he should show them—reason
  To keep a matter hid,
And subtly lead the questions
  Away from what he did.

Thou mirror of uprightness,
  What ails thee at thy vows?
What means the risen whiteness
  Of the skin between thy brows?

GEHAZI

The boils that shine and burrow,
  The sores that slough and bleed–
The leprosy of Naaman
  On thee and all thy seed?
    Stand up, stand up, Gehazi,
      Draw close thy robe and go,
    Gehazi, Judge in Israel,
      A leper white as snow!

THE VIRGINITY

Try as he will, no man breaks wholly loose
From his first love, no matter who she be.
Oh, was there ever sailor free to choose,
That didn't settle somewhere near the sea?

Myself, it don't excite me nor amuse
To watch a pack o' shipping on the sea,
But I can understand my neighbour's views
From certain things which have occurred to me.

Men must keep touch with things they used to use
To earn their living, even when they are free;
And so come back upon the least excuse—
Same as the sailor settled near the sea.

He knows he's never going on no cruise—
He knows he's done and finished with the sea;
And yet he likes to feel she's there to use—
If he should ask her—as she used to be.

THE VIRGINITY

Even though she cost him all he had to lose,
Even though she made him sick to hear or see,
Still, what she left of him will mostly choose
Her skirts to sit by.   How comes such to be?

Parsons in pulpits, tax-payers in pews,
Kings on your thrones, you know as well as me,
We've only one virginity to lose,
And where we lost it there our hearts will be!

A PILGRIM'S WAY

I do not look for holy saints to guide me on my way,
Or male and female devilkins to lead my feet astray.
If these are added, I rejoice—if not, I shall not mind,
So long as I have leave and choice to meet my fellow-kind.
  For as we come and as we go (and deadly-soon go we!)
  The people, Lord, Thy people, are good enough for me!

Thus I will honour pious men whose virtue shines so bright
(Though none are more amazed than I when I by chance do right),
And I will pity foolish men for woe their sins have bred
(Though ninety-nine per cent. of mine I brought on my own head).
  And, Amorite or Eremite, or General Averagee,
  The people, Lord, Thy people, are good enough for me!

A PILGRIM'S WAY

And when they bore me overmuch, I will not shake
 mine ears,
Recalling many thousand such whom I have bored
 to tears.
And when they labour to impress, I will not doubt
 nor scoff;
Since I myself have done no less and—sometimes
 pulled it off.
  Yea, as we are and we are not, and we pretend
    to be,
  The people, Lord, Thy people, are good enough
    for me!

And when they work me random wrong, as often-
 times hath been,
I will not cherish hate too long (my hands are none
 too clean).
And when they do me random good I will not feign
 surprise,
No more than those whom I have cheered with
 wayside charities.

THE YEARS BETWEEN

But, as we give and as we take—whate'er our
    takings be—
The people, Lord, Thy people, are good enough
    for me!

But when I meet with frantic folk who sinfully
    declare
There is no pardon for their sin, the same I will
    not spare
Till I have proved that Heaven and Hell which in
    our hearts we have
Show nothing irredeemable on either side the grave.
    For as we live and as we die—if utter Death
        there be—
    The people, Lord, Thy people, are good enough
        for me!

A PILGRIM'S WAY

Deliver me from every pride—the Middle, High, and Low—
That bars me from a brother's side, whatever pride he show.
And purge me from all heresies of thought and speech and pen
That bid me judge him otherwise than I am judged. *Amen!*

  That I may sing of Crowd or King or road-borne company,
  That I may labour in my day, vocation and degree,

To prove the same in deed and name, and hold unshakenly
(Where'er I go, whate'er I know, whoe'er my neighbour be)
This single faith in Life and Death and all Eternity:
'The people, Lord, Thy people, are good enough for me!'

THE OLDEST SONG

(For before Eve was Lilith.—*Old Tale.*)

THESE were never your true love's eyes.
   Why do you feign that you love them?
You that broke from their constancies,
   And the wide calm brows above them!

This was never your true love's speech.
   Why do you thrill when you hear it?
You that have ridden out of its reach
   The width of the world or near it!

This was never your true love's hair,—
   You that chafed when it bound you
Screened from knowledge or shame or care,
   In the night that it made around you!

'*All these things I know, I know.*
   And that's why my heart is breaking!'
Then what do you gain by pretending so?
   '*The joy of an old wound waking.*'

NATURAL THEOLOGY

PRIMITIVE

I ATE my fill of a whale that died
    And stranded after a month at sea. . . .
There is a pain in my inside.
    Why have the Gods afflicted me?
Ow! I am purged till I am a wraith!
    Wow! I am sick till I cannot see!
What is the sense of Religion and Faith?
    Look how the Gods have afflicted me!

PAGAN

How can the skin of rat or mouse hold
    Anything more than a harmless flea? . . .
The burning plague has taken my household.
    Why have my Gods afflicted me?
All my kith and kin are deceased,
    Though they were as good as good could be
I will out and batter the family priest,
    Because my Gods have afflicted me.

THE YEARS BETWEEN

MEDI EVAL

My privy and well drain into each other
  After the custom of Christendie. . . .
Fevers and fluxes are wasting my mother.
  Why has the Lord afflicted me?
The Saints are helpless for all I offer—
  So are the clergy I used to fee.
Henceforward I keep my cash in my coffer,
  Because the Lord has afflicted me.

MATERIAL

I run eight hundred hens to the acre.
  They die by dozens mysteriously. . . .
I am more than doubtful concerning my Maker
  Why has the Lord afflicted me?
What a return for all my endeavour—
  Not to mention the L. S. D.!
I am an atheist now and for ever,
  Because this God has afflicted me!

PROGRESSIVE

Money spent on an Army or Fleet
  Is homicidal lunacy. . . .

NATURAL THEOLOGY

My son has been killed in the Mons retreat.
　Why is the Lord afflicting me?
Why are murder, pillage and arson
　And rape allowed by the Deity?
I will write to the *Times*, deriding our parson
Because my God has afflicted me.

CHORUS

We had a kettle: we let it leak:
　Our not repairing it made it worse.
We haven't had any tea for a week. . . .
　The bottom is out of the Universe!

CONCLUSION

This was none of the good Lord's pleasure,
　For the Spirit He breathed in Man is free;
But what comes after is measure for measure,
　And not a God that afflicteth thee.
As was the sowing so the reaping
　Is now and evermore shall be.
Thou art delivered to thy own keeping.
　Only Thyself hath afflicted thee!

A SONG AT COCK-CROW

('*Ille autem iterum negavit.*')

THE first time that Peter deniéd his Lord
He shrank from the cudgel, the scourge and the cord,
But followed far off to see what they would do,
Till the cock crew—till the cock crew—
After Gethsemane, till the cock crew!

The first time that Peter deniéd his Lord
'Twas only a maid in the palace who heard,
As he sat by the fire and warmed himself through.
Then the cock crew! Then the cock crew
('Thou also art one of them.')   Then the cock crew!

The first time that Peter deniéd his Lord
He had neither the Throne, nor the Keys nor the Sword—
A poor silly fisherman, what could he do
When the cock crew—when the cock crew—
But weep for his wickedness when the cock crew?

. . . .

A SONG AT COCK-CROW

The next time that Peter deniéd his Lord
He was Fisher of Men, as foretold by the Word,
With the Crown on his brow and the Cross on his
 shoe,
When the cock crew—when the cock crew—
In Flanders and Picardy when the cock crew.

The next time that Peter deniéd his Lord
'Twas Mary the Mother in Heaven Who heard,
And She grieved for the maidens and wives that
 they slew
When the cock crew—when the cock crew—
At Tirmonde and Aerschott when the cock crew.

The next time that Peter deniéd his Lord
The Babe in the Manger awakened and stirred,
And He stretched out His arms for the playmates
 He knew—
When the cock crew—when the cock crew—
But the waters had covered them when the cock crew.

THE YEARS BETWEEN

The next time that Peter denièd his Lord
'Twas Earth in her agony waited his word,
But he sat by the fire and naught would he do,
Though the cock crew—though the cock crew—
Over all Christendom, though the cock crew.

The last time that Peter denièd his Lord,
The Father took from him the Keys and the Sword,
And the Mother and Babe brake his Kingdom in two,
When the cock crew—when the cock crew—
(Because of his wickedness) when the cock crew!

THE FEMALE OF THE SPECIES
1911

When the Himalayan peasant meets the he-bear in his pride,
He shouts to scare the monster, who will often turn aside.
But the she-bear thus accosted rends the peasant tooth and nail.
For the female of the species is more deadly than the male.

When Nag the basking cobra hears the careless foot of man,
He will sometimes wriggle sideways and avoid it as he can.
But his mate makes no such motion where she camps beside the trail.
For the female of the species is more deadly than the male.

THE YEARS BETWEEN

When the early Jesuit fathers preached to Hurons
 and Choctaws,
They prayed to be delivered from the vengeance of
 the squaws.
'Twas the women, not the warriors, turned those
 stark enthusiasts pale.
For the female of the species is more deadly than
 the male.

Man's timid heart is burstnig with the things he
 must not say,
For the Woman that God gave him isn't his to
 give away;
But when hunter meets with husband, each con-
 firms the other's tale—
The female of the species is more deadly than the
 male.

Man, a bear in most relations—worm and savage
 otherwise,—
Man propounds negotiations, Man accepts the com-
 promise.

THE FEMALE OF THE SPECIES

Very rarely will he squarely push the logic of a fact
To its ultimate conclusion in unmitigated act.

Fear, or foolishness, impels him, ere he lay the wicked low,
To concede some form of trial even to his fiercest foe.
Mirth obscene diverts his anger! Doubt and Pity oft perplex
Him in dealing with an issue—to the scandal of The Sex!

But the Woman that God gave him, every fibre of her frame
Proves her launched for one sole issue, armed and engined for the same;
And to serve that single issue, lest the generations fail,
The female of the species must be deadlier than the male.

THE YEARS BETWEEN

She who faces Death by torture for each life beneath her breast
May not deal in doubt or pity—must not swerve for fact or jest.
These be purely male diversions—not in these her honour dwells.
She the Other Law we live by, is that Law and nothing else.

She can bring no more to living than the powers that make her great
As the Mother of the Infant and the Mistress of the Mate!
And when Babe and Man are lacking and she strides unclaimed to claim
Her right as femme (and baron), her equipment is the same.

She is wedded to convictions—in default of grosser ties;
Her contentions are her children, Heaven help him who denies!—

THE FEMALE OF THE SPECIES

He will meet no suave discussion, but the instant, white-hot, wild,
Wakened female of the species warring as for spouse and child.

Unprovoked and awful charges—even so the she-bear fights,
Speech that drips, corrodes, and poisons—even so the cobra bites,
Scientific vivisection of one nerve till it is raw
And the victim writhes in anguish—like the Jesuit with the squaw!

So it comes that Man the coward, when he gathers to confer
With his fellow-braves in council, dare not leave a place for her
Where, at war with Life and Conscience, he uplifts his erring hands
To some God of Abstract Justice—which no woman understands.

THE YEARS BETWEEN

And Man knows it! Knows, moreover, that the
  Woman that God gave him
Must command but may not govern—shall enthral
  but not enslave him.
And *She* knows, because She warns him and Her
  instincts never fail,
That the Female of Her Species is more deadly
  than the Male.

EPITAPHS

'EQUALITY OF SACRIFICE'

A. 'I was a "have."'   *B.* 'I was a "have-not."'
(*Together*). 'What hast thou given which I gave
  not?'

A SERVANT

We were together since the War began.
He was my servant—and the better man.

A SON

My son was killed while laughing at some jest. I
  would I knew
What it was, and it might serve me in a time when
  jests are few.

AN ONLY SON

I have slain none except my Mother. She
(Blessing her slayer) died of grief for me.

THE YEARS BETWEEN

Ex-Clerk

Pity not! The Army gave
Freedom to a timid slave:
In which Freedom did he find
Strength of body, will, and mind:
By which strength he came to prove
Mirth, Companionship, and Love:
For which Love to Death he went:
In which Death he lies content.

The Wonder

Body and Spirit I surrendered whole
To harsh Instructors—and received a soul . . .
If mortal man could change me through and through
From all I was—what may The God not do?

Hindu Sepoy in France

This man in his own country prayed we know not to what Powers.
We pray Them to reward him for his bravery in ours.

EPITAPHS

The Coward

I could not look on Death, which being known,
Men led me to him, blindfold and alone.

Shock

My name, my speech, my self I had forgot.
My wife and children came—I knew them not.
I died. My Mother followed. At her call
And on her bosom I remembered all.

A Grave Near Cairo

Gods of the Nile, should this stout fellow here
Get out—get out! He knows not shame nor fear.

Pelicans in the Wilderness
(a grave near halfa)

The blown sand heaps on me, that none may learn
   Where I am laid for whom my children grieve. . . .
O wings that beat at dawning, ye return
   Out of the desert to your young at eve!

THE YEARS BETWEEN

The Favour

Death favoured me from the first, well knowing I
  could not endure
  To wait on him day by day. He quitted my
  betters and came
Whistling over the fields, and, when he had made
  all sure,
  'Thy line is at end,' he said, 'but at least I have
  saved its name.'

The Beginner

On the first hour of my first day
  In the front trench I fell.
(Children in boxes at a play
  Stand up to watch it well.)

R. A. F. (Aged Eighteen)

Laughing through clouds, his milk-teeth still un-
  shed,
Cities and men he smote from overhead.
His deaths delivered, he returned to play
Childlike, with childish things now put away.

EPITAPHS

THE REFINED MAN

I was of delicate mind. I went aside for my needs,
  Disdaining the common office. I was seen from afar and killed. . . .
How is this matter for mirth? Let each man be judged by his deeds.
  I have paid my price to live with myself on the terms that I willed.

NATIVE WATER-CARRIER (M. E. F.)

Prometheus brought down fire to men.
  This brought up water.
The Gods are jealous—now, as then,
  They gave no quarter.

BOMBED IN LONDON

On land and sea I strove with anxious care
To escape conscription. It was in the air!

THE YEARS BETWEEN

THE SLEEPY SENTINEL

Faithless the watch that I kept: now I have none to keep.
I was slain because I slept: now I am slain I sleep.
Let no man reproach me again, whatever watch is unkept—
I sleep because I am slain. They slew me because I slept.

BATTERIES OUT OF AMMUNITION

If any mourn us in the workshop, say
We died because the shift kept holiday

COMMON FORM

If any question why we died,
Tell them, because our fathers lied.

A DEAD STATESMAN

I could not dig: I dared not rob:
Therefore I lied to please the mob.
Now all my lies are proved untrue,
And I must face the men I slew.
What tale shall save me here among
Mine angry and defrauded young?

EPITAPHS

The Rebel

If I had clamoured at Thy Gate
  For gift of Life on Earth,
And, thrusting through the souls that wait
  Flung headlong into birth—
Even then, even then, for gin and snare
  About my pathway spread,
Lord, I had mocked Thy thoughtful care
  Before I joined the Dead!
But now? . . . I was beneath Thy Hand
  Ere yet the Planets came.
And now—though Planets pass, I stand
  The witness to Thy Shame.

The Obedient

Daily, though no ears attended,
  Did my prayers arise.
Daily, though no fire descended
  Did I sacrifice. . . .
Though my darkness did not lift,
  Though I faced no lighter odds,
Though the Gods bestowed no gift,
      None the less,
  None the less, I served the Gods!

THE YEARS BETWEEN

A Drifter off Tarentum

He from the wind-bitten north with ship and companions descended,
　Searching for eggs of death spawned by invisible hulls.
Many he found and drew forth. Of a sudden the fishery ended
　In flame and a clamorous breath not new to the eye-pecking gulls.

Destroyers in Collision

　For Fog and Fate no charm is found
　　To lighten or amend.
　I, hurrying to my bride, was drowned—
　　Cut down by my best friend.

Convoy Escort

I was a shepherd to fools
　Causelessly bold or afraid.
They would not abide by my rules.
　Yet they escaped. For I stayed.

EPITAPHS

Unknown Female Corpse

Headless, lacking foot and hand,
Horrible I come to land.
I beseech all women's sons
Know I was a mother once.

Raped and Revenged

One used and butchered me: another spied
Me broken—for which thing a hundred died
So it was learned among the heathen hosts
How much a freeborn woman's favour costs

Salonikan Grave

I have watched a thousand days
Push out and crawl into night
Slowly as tortoises.
Now I, too, follow these.
It is fever, and not fight—
Time, not battle—that slays.

THE YEARS BETWEEN

The Bridegroom

Call me not false, beloved,
  If, from thy scarce-known breast
So little time removed,
  In other arms I rest.

For this more ancient bride
  Whom coldly I embrace
Was constant at my side
  Before I saw thy face.

Our marriage, often set—
  By miracle delayed—
At last is consummate,
  And cannot be unmade.

Live, then, whom Life shall cure,
  Almost, of Memory,
And leave us to endure
  Its immortality.

EPITAPHS

V. A. D. (Mediterranean)

Ah, would swift ships had never been, for then we ne'er had found,
These harsh Egean rocks between, this little virgin drowned,
Whom neither spouse nor child shall mourn, but men she nursed through pain
And—certain keels for whose return the heathen look in vain.

'THE CITY OF BRASS'
1909

'Here was a people whom after their works thou shalt see wept over for their lost dominion: and in this palace is the last information respecting lords collected in the dust.'—*The Arabian Nights.*

I<small>N</small> *a land that the sand overlays—the ways to her gates are untrod—*
A multitude ended their days whose fates were made splendid by God,
Till they grew drunk and were smitten with madness and went to their fall,
And of these is a story written: but Allah alone knoweth all!

When the wine stirred in their heart their bosoms dilated,
They rose to suppose themselves kings over all things created—
To decree a new earth at a birth without labour or sorrow—
To declare: 'We prepare it to-day and inherit to-morrow.'

THE CITY OF BRASS'

They chose themselves prophets and priests of minute understanding,
Men swift to see done, and outrun, their extremest commanding—
Of the tribe which describe with a jibe the perversions of Justice—
Panders avowed to the crowd whatsoever its lust is.

Swiftly these pulled down the walls that their fathers had made them—
The impregnable ramparts of old, they razed and relaid them
As playgrounds of pleasure and leisure with limitless entries,
And havens of rest for the wastrels where once walked the sentries;
And because there was need of more pay for the shouters and marchers,
They disbanded in face of their foemen their bowmen and archers.
They replied to their well-wishers' fears—to their enemies' laughter,
Saying: 'Peace! We have fashioned a God Which shall save us hereafter.

THE YEARS BETWEEN

We ascribe all dominion to man in his factions conferring,
And have given to numbers the Name of the Wisdom unerring.'
They said: 'Who has hate in his soul? Who has envied his neighbour?
Let him arise and control both that man and his labour.'

They said: 'Who is eaten by sloth? Whose unthrift has destroyed him?
He shall levy a tribute from all because none have employed him.'
They said: 'Who hath toiled? Who hath striven, and gathered possession?
Let him be spoiled. He hath given full proof of transgression.'
They said: 'Who is irked by the Law? *Though we may not remove it,*
If he lend us his aid in this raid, we will set him above it!'
So the robber did judgment again upon such as displeased him,
The slayer, too, boasted his slain, and the judges released him.

'THE CITY OF BRASS'

As for their kinsmen far off, on the skirts of the nation,
They harried all earth to make sure none escaped reprobation.
They awakened unrest for a jest in their newly-won borders,
And jeered at the blood of their brethren betrayed by their orders.
They instructed the ruled to rebel, their rulers to aid them;
And, since such as obeyed them not fell, their Viceroys obeyed them.
When the riotous set them at naught they said: 'Praise the upheaval!
For the show and the word and the thought of Dominion is evil!'

They unwound and flung from them with rage, as a rag that defiled them
The imperial gains of the age which their forefathers piled them.
They ran panting in haste to lay waste and embitter for ever

THE YEARS BETWEEN

The wellsprings of Wisdom and Strength which are
 Faith and Endeavour.
They nosed out and digged up and dragged forth
 and exposed to derision
All doctrine of purpose and worth and restraint
 and prevision:
And it ceased, and God granted them all things
 for which they had striven,
And the heart of a beast in the place of a man's
 heart was given. . . .
. . . . . .

When they were fullest of wine and most flagrant
 in error,
Out of the sea rose a sign—out of Heaven a terror.
Then they saw, then they heard, then they knew—
 for none troubled to hide it,
An host had prepared their destruction, but still
 they denied it.
They denied what they dared not abide if it came
 to the trial,
But the Sword that was forged while they lied did
 not heed their denial.
It drove home, and no time was allowed to the
 crowd that was driven.

'THE CITY OF BRASS'

The preposterous-minded were cowed—they thought time would be given.
There was no need of a steed nor a lance to pursue them;
It was decreed their own deed, and not chance, should undo them.
The tares they had laughingly sown were ripe to the reaping,
The trust they had leagued to disown was removed from their keeping.
The eaters of other men's bread, the exempted from hardship,
The excusers of impotence fled, abdicating their wardship.
For the hate they had taught through the State brought the State no defender,
And it passed from the roll of the Nations in headlong surrender.

JUSTICE

October 1918

Across a world where all men grieve
  And grieving strive the more,
The great days range like tides and leave
  Our dead on every shore.
Heavy the load we undergo,
  And our own hands prepare,
If we have parley with the foe,
  The load our sons must bear.

Before we loose the word
  That bids new worlds to birth,
Needs must we loosen first the sword
  Of Justice upon earth;
Or else all else is vain
  Since life on earth began,
And the spent world sinks back again
  Hopeless of God and Man.

JUSTICE

A people and their King
  Through ancient sin grown strong,
Because they feared no reckoning
  Would set no bound to wrong;
But now their hour is past,
  And we who bore it find
Evil Incarnate held at last
  To answer to mankind.

For agony and spoil
  Of nations beat to dust,
For poisoned air and tortured soil
  And cold, commanded lust,
And every secret woe
  The shuddering waters saw—
Willed and fulfilled by high and low—
  Let them relearn the Law.

That when the dooms are read,
  Not high nor low shall say:—
'My haughty or my humble head
  Has saved me in this day.'

THE YEARS BETWEEN

That, till the end of time,
  Their remnant shall recall
Their fathers' old, confederate crime
  Availed them not at all.

That neither schools nor priests,
  Nor Kings may build again
A people with the heart of beasts
  Made wise concerning men.
Whereby our dead shall sleep
  In honour, unbetrayed,
And we in faith and honour keep
  That peace for which they paid.

POEMS FROM HISTORY

THE RIVER'S TALE

Prehistoric

Twenty bridges from Tower to Kew
Wanted to know what the River knew,
For they were young and the Thames was old,
And this is the tale that the River told:—

'I walk my beat before London Town,
Five hours up and seven down.
Up I go and I end my run
At Tide-end-town, which is Teddington.
Down I come with the mud in my hands
And plaster it over the Maplin Sands.
But I'd have you know that these waters of mine
Were once a branch of the River Rhine,
When hundreds of miles to the East I went
And England was joined to the Continent.

I remember the bat-winged lizard-birds,
The Age of Ice and the mammoth herds,
And the giant tigers that stalked them down
Through Regent's Park into Camden Town.

POEMS FROM HISTORY

And I remember like yesterday
The earliest Cockney who came my way,
When he pushed through the forest that lined the Strand,
With paint on his face and a club in his hand.
He was death to feather and fin and fur,
He trapped my beavers at Westminster,
He netted my salmon, he hunted my deer,
He killed my herons off Lambeth Pier;
He fought his neighbour with axes and swords,
Flint or bronze, at my upper fords,
While down at Greenwich for slaves and tin
The tall Phoenician ships stole in,
And North Sea war-boats, painted and gay,
Flashed like dragon-flies Erith way;
And Norseman and Negro and Gaul and Greek
Drank with the Britons in Barking Creek,
And life was gay, and the world was new,
And I was a mile across at Kew!
But the Roman came with a heavy hand,
And bridged and roaded and ruled the land,
And the Roman left and the Danes blew in—
And that's where your history books begin!'

THE ROMAN CENTURION SPEAKS
A. D. 300

Legate, I had the news last night. My cohort's ordered home
By ship to Portus Itius and thence by road to Rome.
I've marched the companies aboard, the arms are stowed below:
Now let another take my sword. Command me not to go!

I've served in Britain forty years, from Vectis to the Wall
I have none other home than this, nor any life at all.
Last night I did not understand, but, now the hour draws near
That calls me to my native land, I feel that land is here.

POEMS FROM HISTORY

Here where men say my name was made, here
    where my work was done,
Here where my dearest dead are laid—my wife—
    my wife and son;
Here where time, custom, grief and toil, age, memory, service, love,
Have rooted me in British soil. Ah, how shall I
    remove?

For me this land, that sea, these airs, those folk
    and fields suffice.
What purple Southern pomp can match our changeful Northern skies,
Black with December snows unshed or pearled
    with August haze,
The clanging arch of steel-grey March, or June's
    long-lighted days?

You'll follow widening Rhodanus till vine and
    olive lean
Aslant before the sunny breeze that sweeps Nemausus clean
To Arelate's triple gate; but let me linger on,
Here where our stiff-necked British oaks confront
    Euroclydon!

THE ROMAN CENTURION SPEAKS

You'll take the old Aurelian Road through shore-descending pines
Where, blue as any peacock's neck, the Tyrrhene Ocean shines.
You'll go where laurel crowns are won, but will you e'er forget
The scent of hawthorn in the sun, or bracken in the wet?

Let me work here for Britain's sake—at any task you will—
A marsh to drain, a road to make or native troops to drill.
Some Western camp (I know the Pict) or granite Border keep,
Mid seas of heather derelict, where our old messmates sleep.

Legate, I come to you in tears—My cohort ordered home!
I've served in Britain forty years. What should I do in Rome?

POEMS FROM HISTORY

Here is my heart, my soul, my mind—the only life I know.—
I cannot leave it all behind. Command me not to go!

THE PIRATES IN ENGLAND

A. D. 600

When Rome was rotten-ripe to her fall,
  And the sceptre passed from her hand,
The pestilent Picts leaped over the wall
  To harry the British land.

The little dark men of the mountain and waste,
  So quick to laughter and tears,
They came panting with hate and haste
  For the loot of five hundred years.

They killed the trader, they sacked the shops,
  They ruined temple and town—
They swept like wolves through the standing crops
  Crying that Rome was down.

They wiped out all that they could find
  Of beauty and strength and worth,
But they could not wipe out the Viking's Wind,
  That brings the ships from the North.

POEMS FROM HISTORY

They could not wipe out the North-East gales,
   Nor what those gales set free—
The pirate ships with their close-reefed sails,
   Leaping from sea to sea.

They had forgotten the shield-hung hull
   Seen nearer and more plain,
Dipping into the troughs like a gull,
   And gull-like rising again—

The painted eyes that glare and frown,
   In the high snake-headed stem,
Searching the beach while her sail comes down,
   They had forgotten them!

There was no Count of the Saxon Shore
   To meet her hand to hand,
As she took the beach with a surge and a roar,
   And the pirates rushed inland.

DANE-GELD

A. D. 1000

It is always a temptation to an armed and agile nation,
  To call upon a neighbour and to say:—
'We invaded you last night—we are quite prepared to fight,
Unless you pay us cash to go away.'

   And that is called asking for Dane-geld,
     And the people who ask it explain
   That you've only to pay 'em the Dane-geld
     And then you'll get rid of the Dane!

It is always a temptation to a rich and lazy nation,
  To puff and look important and to say:—
'Though we know we should defeat you, we have not the time to meet you,
We will therefore pay you cash to go away.'

POEMS FROM HISTORY

And that is called paying the Dane-geld;
  But we've proved it again and again,
That if once you have paid him the Dane-geld
  You never get rid of the Dane.

It is wrong to put temptation in the path of any
    nation,
  For fear they should succumb and go astray,
So when you are requested to pay up or be molested,
  You will find it better policy to say:—

'We never pay any one Dane-geld,
  No matter how trifling the cost,
For the end of that game is oppression and
    shame,
  And the nation that plays it is lost!'

THE MAKING OF ENGLAND

(WILLIAM THE CONQUEROR)

ENGLAND's on the anvil—hear the hammers ring—
  Clanging from the Severn to the Tyne!
Never was a blacksmith like our Norman King—
  England's being hammered, hammered, hammered into line!

England's on the anvil! Heavy are the blows!
  (But the work will be a marvel when it's done)
Little bits of Kingdoms cannot stand against their foes.
  England's being hammered, hammered, hammered into one!

There shall be one people—it shall serve one Lord—
  (Neither Priest nor Baron shall escape!)
It shall have one speech and law, soul and strength and sword.
  England's being hammered, hammered, hammered into shape!

NORMAN AND SAXON

A. D. 1120

'My son,' said the Norman Baron, 'I am dying, and you will be heir
To all the broad acres in England that William gave me for my share
When we conquered the Saxon at Hastings, and a nice little handful it is.
But before you go over to rule it I want you to understand this:—

'The Saxon is not like us Normans. His manners are not so polite,
But he never means anything serious till he talks about justice and right;
When he stands like an ox in the furrow with his sullen set eyes on your own,
And grumbles, "This isn't fair dealing," my son, leave the Saxon alone.

NORMAN AND SAXON

'You can horsewhip your Gascony archers, or torture your Picardy spears,
But don't try that game on the Saxon; you'll have the whole brood round your ears.
From the richest old Thane in the county to the poorest chained serf in the fields,
They'll be at you and on you like hornets, and, if you are wise, you will yield!

'But first you must master their language, their dialect, proverbs and songs,
Don't trust any clerk to interpret when they come with the tale of their wrongs.
Let them know that you know what they're saying; let them feel that you know what to say;
Yes, even when you want to go hunting, hear them out if it takes you all day.

'They'll drink every hour of the daylight and poach every hour of the dark,
It's the sport not the rabbits they're after (we've plenty of game in the park).

POEMS FROM HISTORY

Don't hang them or cut off their fingers. That's wasteful as well as unkind,
For a hard-bitten, South-country poacher makes the best man-at-arms you can find.

'Appear with your wife and the children at their weddings and funerals and feasts;
Be polite but not friendly to Bishops; be good to all poor parish priests;
Say "we", "us" and "ours" when you're talking instead of "*you fellows*" and "*I*".
Don't ride over seeds; keep your temper; and *never you tell 'em a lie!*'

THE REEDS OF RUNNYMEDE

(MAGNA CHARTA, JUNE 15, 1215)

AT Runnymede, at Runnymede,
  What say the reeds at Runnymede?
The lissom reeds that give and take,
That bend so far, but never break,
They keep the sleepy Thames awake
  With tales of John at Runnymede.

At Runnymede, at Runnymede,
  Oh hear the reeds at Runnymede:—
'You mustn't sell, delay, deny,
A freeman's right or liberty,
It wakes the stubborn Englishry,
  We saw 'em roused at Runnymede!

'When through our ranks the Barons came,
With little thought of praise or blame,
But resolute to play the game,
  They lumbered up to Runnymede;

POEMS FROM HISTORY

And there they launched in solid line,
The first attack on Right Divine—
The curt, uncompromising "Sign!"
   That settled John at Runnymede.

'At Runnymede, at Runnymede,
Your rights were won at Runnymede!
No freeman shall be fined or bound,
   Or dispossessed of freehold ground,
Except by lawful judgement found
And passed upon him by his peers!—
Forget not, after all these years,
   The charter signed at Runnymede.'

And still when mob or monarch lays
Too rude a hand on English ways,
The whisper wakes, the shudder plays,
   Across the reeds at Runnymede.
And Thames, that knows the moods of kings,
And crowds and priests and suchlike things,
Rolls deep and dreadful as he brings
   Their warning down from Runnymede!

MY FATHER'S CHAIR

(THE FIRST PARLIAMENT)

THERE are four good legs to my Father's Chair—
Priest and People and Lords and Crown.
I sit on all of 'em fair and square,
And that is the reason it don't break down.

I won't trust one leg, nor two, nor three,
To carry my weight when I sit me down,
I want all four of 'em under me—
Priest and People and Lords and Crown.

I sit on all four and I favour none—
Priest, nor People, nor Lords, nor Crown—
And I never tilt in my chair, my son,
And that is the reason it don't break down!

When your time comes to sit in my Chair,
Remember your Father's habits and rules,
Sit on all four legs, fair and square,
And never be tempted by one-legged stools!

THE DAWN WIND

(ON THE EVE OF THE RENAISSANCE)

AT two o'clock in the morning, if you open your window and listen,
 You will hear the feet of the Wind that is going to call the sun.
And the trees in the shadow rustle and the trees in the moonlight glisten,
 And though it is deep, dark night, you feel that the night is done.

So do the cows in the field. They graze for an hour and lie down,
 Dozing and chewing the cud; or a bird in the ivy wakes,
Chirrups one note and is still, and the restless Wind strays on,
 Fidgeting far down the road, till, softly, the darkness breaks.

THE DAWN WIND

Back comes the Wind full strength with a blow like an angel's wing,
  Gentle but waking the world, as he shouts: 'The Sun! The Sun!'
And the light floods over the fields and the birds begin to sing,
  And the Wind dies down in the grass. It is Day and his work is done.

So when the world is asleep, and there seems no hope of her waking
  Out of some long, bad dream that makes her mutter and moan,
Suddenly, all men arise to the noise of fetters breaking,
  And every one smiles at his neighbour and tells him his soul is his own!

THE KING'S JOB

(THE TUDORS)

Once on a time was a King anxious to understand
What was the wisest thing a man could do for his land.
Most of his population hurried to answer the question,
Each with a long oration, each with a new suggestion.
They interrupted his meals, he wasn't safe in his bed from 'em,
They hung round his neck and heels, and at last His Majesty fled from 'em.
He put on a leper's cloak (people leave lepers alone),
Out of the window he broke, and abdicated his throne.
All that rapturous day, while his Court and his Ministers mourned him,
He danced on his own highway till his own Policemen warned him.

THE KING'S JOB

Gay and cheerful he ran (lepers don't cheer as a rule)
Till he found a philosopher-man teaching an infant school.
The windows were open wide, the King sat down on the grass,
And heard the children inside reciting 'Our King is an ass.'
The King popped in his head, 'Some people would call this treason,
But I think you are right,' he said; 'will you kindly give me your reason?'
Lepers in school are rare as kings with a leper's dress on,
But the class didn't stop or stare; it calmly went on with the lesson:
'The wisest thing, we suppose, that a man can do for his land,
Is the work that lies under his nose, with the tools that lie under his hand.'
The King whipped off his cloak, and stood in his crown before 'em.
He said:—'My dear little folk, *Ex ore parvulorum*

POEMS FROM HISTORY

(Which is Latin for "Children know more than grown-ups would credit")
You have shown me the road to go, and I propose to tread it.'
Back to his Kingdom he ran, and issued a Proclamation,
'Let every living man return to his occupation!'
Then he explained to the mob that cheered in his palace and round it,
'I've been to look for a job, and Heaven be praised I've found it!'

WITH DRAKE IN THE TROPICS

South and far south below the Line,
  Our Admiral leads us on,
Above, undreamed-of planets shine—
  The stars we knew are gone.
Around, our clustered seamen mark
  The silent deep ablaze
With fires, through which the far-down shark
  Shoots glimmering on his ways.

The sultry tropic breezes fail
  That plagued us all day through;
Like molten silver hangs our sail,
  Our decks are dark with dew.
Now the rank moon commands the sky,
  Ho! Bid the watch beware
And rouse all sleeping men that lie
  Unsheltered in her glare.

How long the time 'twixt bell and bell!
  How still our lanthorns burn!
How strange our whispered words that tell
  Of England and return!

POEMS FROM HISTORY

Old towns, old streets, old friends, old loves,
    We name them each to each,
While the lit face of Heaven removes
    Them farther from our reach.

Now is the utmost ebb of night
    When mind and body sink,
And loneliness and gathering fright
    O'erwhelm us, if we think—
Yet, look, where in his room apart,
    All windows opened wide,
Our Admiral thrusts away the chart
    And comes to walk outside.

Kindly, from man to man he goes,
    With comfort, praise, or jest,
Quick to suspect our childish woes,
    Our terror and unrest.
It is as though the sun should shine—
    Our midnight fears are gone!
South and far south below the Line,
    Our Admiral leads us on!

'TOGETHER'

(ELIZABETH AND HER PEOPLE)

When Horse and Rider each can trust the other everywhere,
It takes a fence and more than a fence to pound that happy pair;
For the one will do what the other demands, although he is beaten and blown,
And when it is done, they can live through a run that neither could face alone.

When Crew and Captain understand each other to the core,
It takes a gale and more than a gale to put their ship ashore;
For the one will do what the other commands, although they are chilled to the bone,
And both together can live through weather that neither could face alone.

POEMS FROM HISTORY

When King and People understand each other past
    a doubt,
It takes a foe and more than a foe to knock that
    country out;
For the one will do what the other one asks as soon
    as the need is known,
And hand in hand they can make a stand which
    neither could make alone!

This wisdom had Elizabeth and all her subjects too,
For she was theirs and they were hers, as well the
    Spaniard knew;
For when his grim Armada came to conquer the
    Nation and Throne,
Why, back to back they met an attack that neither
    could face alone!

It is not wealth nor talk nor trade nor schools nor
    even the Vote,
Will save your land when the enemy's hand is
    tightening round your throat.

'TOGETHER'

But a King and a People who thoroughly trust
   each other in all that is done
Can sleep on their bed without any dread—for the
   world will leave 'em alone!

(KING JAMES I)

THE child of Mary Queen of Scots,
   A shifty mother's shiftless son,
Bred up among intrigues and plots,
   Learnèd in all things, wise in none!
Ungainly, babbling, wasteful, weak,
   Shrewd, clever, cowardly, pedantic,
The sight of steel would blanch his cheek,
   The smell of baccy drive him frantic.
He was the author of his line—
   He wrote that witches should be burnt;
He wrote that monarchs were divine,
   And left a son who proved they weren't!

THE CIVIL WARS

(Before Edgehill, October, 1642)

Naked and grey the Cotswolds stand
   Beneath the autumn sun,
And the stubble fields on either hand
   Where Stour and Avon run,
There is no change in the patient land
   That has bred us every one.

She should have passed in cloud and fire
   And saved us from this sin
Of war—red war—'twixt child and sire,
   Household and kith and kin,
In the heart of a sleepy Midland shire,
   With the harvest scarcely in.

But there is no change as we meet at last
   On the brow-head or the plain,
And the raw astonished ranks stand fast
   To slay or to be slain
By the men they knew in the kindly past
   That shall never come again—

THE CIVIL WARS

By the men they met at dance or chase,
   In the tavern or the hall,
At the justice-bench and the market-place,
   At the cudgel-play or brawl,
Of their own blood and speech and race,
   Comrades or neighbours all!

More bitter than death this day must prove
   Whichever way it go,
For the brothers of the maids we love
   Make ready to lay low
Their sisters' sweethearts, as we move
   Against our dearest foe.

Thank Heaven! At last the trumpets peal
   Before our strength gives way.
For King or for the Commonweal
   No matter which they say,
The first dry rattle of new-drawn steel
   Changes the world to-day!

THE DUTCH IN THE MEDWAY

(CHARLES II)

IF war were won by feasting,
 Or victory by song,
Or safety found in sleeping sound,
 How England would be strong!
But honour and dominion
 Are not maintainèd so,
They're only got by sword and shot,
 And this the Dutchmen know!

The moneys that should feed us,
 You spend on your delight,
How can you then have sailor-men
 To aid you in your fight?
Our fish and cheese are rotten,
 Which makes the scurvy grow—
We cannot serve you if we starve,
 And this the Dutchmen know!

THE DUTCH IN THE MEDWAY

Our ships in every harbour
  Be neither whole nor sound,
And, when we seek to mend a leak,
  No oakum can be found,
Or, if it is, the caulkers,
  And carpenters also,
For lack of pay have gone away,
  And this the Dutchmen know!

Mere powder, guns, and bullets,
  We scarce can get at all,
Their price was spent in merriment
  And revel at Whitehall,
While we in tattered doublets
  From ship to ship must row,
Beseeching friends for odds and ends—
  And this the Dutchmen know!

No King will heed our warnings,
  No Court will pay our claims—
Our King and Court for their disport
  Do sell the very Thames!

POEMS FROM HISTORY

For, now De Ruyter's topsails,
    Off naked Chatham show,
We dare not meet him with our fleet—
    And this the Dutchmen know!

'BROWN BESS'

English Army, 1700–1815

In the days of lace-ruffles, perukes and brocade
  Brown Bess was a partner whom none could
    despise—
An out-spoken, flinty-lipped, brazen-faced jade,
  With a habit of looking men straight in the eyes—
At Blenheim and Ramillies fops would confess
They were pierced to the heart by the charms of
    Brown Bess.

Though her sight was not long and her weight was
    not small,
  Yet her actions were winning, her language was
    clear;
And everyone bowed as she opened the ball
  On the arm of some high-gaitered, grim grenadier.
Half Europe admitted the striking success
Of the dances and routs that were given by Brown
    Bess.

POEMS FROM HISTORY

When ruffles were turned into stiff leather stocks
   And people wore pigtails instead of perukes
Brown Bess never altered her iron-grey locks,
   She knew she was valued for more than her looks.
'Oh, powder and patches was always my dress,
And I think I am killing enough,' said Brown Bess.

So she followed her red-coats, whatever they did,
   From the heights of Quebec to the plains of Assaye,
From Gibraltar to Acre, Cape Town and Madrid,
   And nothing about her was changed on the way;
(But most of the Empire which now we possess
Was won through those years by old-fashioned Brown Bess.)

In stubborn retreat or in stately advance,
   From the Portugal coast to the cork-woods of Spain
She had puzzled some excellent Marshals of France
   Till none of them wanted to meet her again:
But later, near Brussels, Napoleon, no less,
Arranged for a Waterloo ball with Brown Bess.

'BROWN BESS'

She had danced till the dawn of that terrible day—
  She danced on till dusk of more terrible night,
And before her linked squares his battalions gave way
  And her long fierce quadrilles put his lancers to flight.
And when his gilt carriage drove off in the press,
'I have danced my last dance for the world!' said Brown Bess.

If you go to Museums—there's one in Whitehall—
  Where old weapons are shown with their names writ beneath,
You will find her, upstanding, her back to the wall,
  As stiff as a ramrod, the flint in her teeth.
And if ever we English have reason to bless
Any arm save our mothers', that arm is Brown Bess!

THE AMERICAN WAR

(BEFORE)

'TWAS not while England's sword unsheathed
  Put half a world to flight,
Nor while their new-built cities breathed
  Secure behind her might;
Not while she poured from Pole to Line
  Treasure and ships and men—
These worshippers at Freedom's shrine
  They did not quit her then!

Not till their foes were driven forth
  By England o'er the main—
Not till the Frenchman from the North
  Had gone, with shattered Spain;
Not till the clean-swept ocean showed
  No hostile flag unrolled,
Did they remember what they owed
  To Freedom—and were bold!

THE AMERICAN WAR

(AFTER)

The snow lies thick on Valley Forge,
   The ice on the Delaware,
But the poor dead soldiers of King George
   They neither know nor care—

Not though the earliest primrose break
   On the sunny side of the lane,
And scuffling rookeries awake
   Their England's spring again.

They will not stir when the drifts are gone
   Or the ice melts out of the bay,
And the men that served with Washington
   Lie all as still as they.

They will not stir though the mayflower blows
   In the moist dark woods of pine,
And every rock-strewn pasture shows
   Mullein and columbine.

POEMS FROM HISTORY

Each for his land, in a fair fight,
  Encountered, strove, and died,
And the kindly earth that knows no spite
  Covers them side by side.

She is too busy to think of war;
  She has all the world to make gay,
And, behold, the yearly flowers are
  Where they were in our fathers' day!

Golden-rod by the pasture wall
  When the columbine is dead,
And sumach leaves that turn, in fall,
  Red as the blood they shed.

THE FRENCH WARS

(NAPOLEONIC)

The boats of Newhaven and Folkestone and Dover
To Dieppe and Boulogne and to Calais cross over;
And in each of those runs there is not a square yard
Where the English and French haven't fought and
    fought hard!

If the ships that were sunk could be floated once
    more,
They'd stretch like a raft from the shore to the
    shore,
And we'd see, as we crossed, every pattern and plan
Of ship that was built since sea-fighting began.

There'd be biremes and brigantines, cutters and
    sloops,
Cogs, carracks and galleons with gay gilded poops—
Hoys, caravels, ketches, corvettes and the rest,
As thick as regattas, from Ramsgate to Brest.

POEMS FROM HISTORY

But the galleys of Caesar, the squadrons of Sluys,
And Nelson's crack frigates are hid from our eyes,
Where the high Seventy-fours of Napoleon's days
Lie down with Deal luggers and French *chasse-marées*.

They'll answer no signal—they rest on the ooze
With their honey-combed guns and their skeleton crews—
And racing above them, through sunshine or gale,
The Cross-Channel packets come in with the Mail.

Then the poor sea-sick passengers, English and French,
Must open their trunks on the Custom-house bench,
While the officers rummage for smuggled cigars
And nobody thinks of our blood-thirsty wars!

THE BELLS AND QUEEN VICTORIA
1911

'Gay go up and gay go down
To ring the Bells of London Town.'
When London Town's asleep in bed
You'll hear the Bells ring overhead,
    In excelsis gloria!
    Ringing for Victoria,
Ringing for their mighty mistress—ten years dead!

Here is more gain than Gloriana guessed,
    Than Gloriana guessed or Indies bring—
Than golden Indies bring. A Queen confessed,
    A Queen confessed that crowned her people King.
Her people King, and crowned all Kings above,
    Above all Kings have crowned their Queen their love—
Have crowned their love their Queen, their Queen their love!

POEMS FROM·HISTORY

Denying her, we do ourselves deny,
  Disowning her are we ourselves disowned.
Mirror was she of our fidelity,
  And handmaid of our destiny enthroned;
The very marrow of Youth's dream, and still
Yoke-mate of wisest Age that worked her will!

Our fathers had declared to us her praise.
  Her praise the years had proven past all speech,
And past all speech our loyal hearts always,
  Always our hearts lay open, each to each;
Therefore men gave their treasure and their blood
To this one woman—for she understood!

Four o' the clock! Now all the world is still.
Oh, London Bells, to all the world declare
The Secret of the Empire—read who will!
The Glory of the People—touch who dare!

THE BELLS:
    Power that has reached itself all kingly powers,
      St. Margaret's : By love o'erpowered—
      St. Martin's : By love o'erpowered—
      St. Clement Danes : By love o'erpowered,
              The greater power confers!

THE BELLS AND QUEEN VICTORIA

THE BELLS:
    For we were hers, as she, as she was ours,
        Bow Bells : And she was ours—
        St. Paul's : And she was ours—
        Westminster : And she was ours,
                As we, even we, were hers!

THE BELLS:
    As we were hers!

BIG STEAMERS

(MODERN WAR)

'Oh, where are you going to, all you Big Steamers,
  With England's own coal, up and down the salt seas?'
'We are going to fetch you your bread and your butter,
  Your beef, pork, and mutton, eggs, apples, and cheese.'

'And where will you fetch it from, all you Big Steamers,
  And where shall I write you when you are away?'
'We fetch it from Melbourne, Quebec, and Vancouver,
  Address us at Hobart, Hong-kong, and Bombay.'

'But if anything happened to all you Big Steamers,
  And suppose you were wrecked up and down the salt sea?'
'Why, you'd have no coffee or bacon for breakfast,
  And you'd have no muffins or toast for your tea.'

BIG STEAMERS

'Then I'll pray for fine weather for all you big
    Steamers,
  For little blue billows and breezes so soft.'
'Oh, billows and breezes don't bother Big Steamers,
  For we're iron below and steel-rigging aloft.'

'Then I'll build a new lighthouse for all you Big
    Steamers,
  With plenty wise pilots to pilot you through.'
'Oh, the Channel's as bright as a ball-room already,
  And pilots are thicker than pilchards at Looe.'

'Then what can I do for you, all you Big Steamers,
  Oh, what can I do for your comfort and good?'
'Send out your big warships to watch your big
    waters,
  That no one may stop us from bringing you food.

'*For the bread that you eat and the biscuits you nibble,*
  The sweets that you suck and the joints that you
    carve,
They are brought to you daily by all us Big Steamers,
  And if any one hinders our coming you'll starve!'

THE SECRET OF THE MACHINES

We were taken from the ore-bed and the mine,
  We were melted in the furnace and the pit—
We were cast and wrought and hammered to design,
  We were cut and filed and tooled and gauged to fit.
Some water, coal, and oil is all we ask,
  And a thousandth of an inch to give us play,
And now if you will set us to our task,
  We will serve you four and twenty hours a day!

    We can pull and haul and push and lift and drive,
    We can print and plough and weave and heat and light,
    We can run and jump and swim and fly and dive,
    We can see and hear and count and read and write!

THE SECRET OF THE MACHINES

Would you call a friend from half across the world?
  If you'll let us have his name and town and state,
You shall see and hear your crackling question hurled
  Across the arch of heaven while you wait.
Has he answered? Does he need you at his side?
  You can start this very evening if you choose,
And take the Western Ocean in the stride
  Of seventy thousand horses and some screws!

    The boat-express is waiting your command!
    You will find the *Mauretania* at the quay,
    Till her captain turns the lever 'neath his hand
    And the monstrous nine-decked city goes to sea.

Do you wish to make the mountains bare their head
  And lay their new-cut forests at your feet?
Do you want to turn a river in its bed,
  And plant a barren wilderness with wheat?
Shall we pipe aloft and bring you water down
  From the never-failing cisterns of the snows,
To work the mills and tramways in your town,
  And irrigate your orchards as it flows?

POEMS FROM HISTORY

    It is easy! Give us dynamite and drills!
    Watch the iron-shouldered rocks lie down and quake
    As the thirsty desert-level floods and fills,
    And the valley we have dammed becomes a lake!

But remember, please, the Law by which we live,
  We are not built to comprehend a lie,
We can neither love nor pity nor forgive,
  If you make a slip in handling us you die!
We are greater than the Peoples or the Kings—
  Be humble, as you crawl beneath our rods!—
Our touch can alter all created things,
  We are everything on earth—except The Gods!

    Though our smoke may hide the Heavens from your eyes,
    It will vanish and the stars will shine again,
    Because, for all our power and weight and size,
    We are nothing more than children of your brain!

THE GLORY OF THE GARDEN

Our England is a garden that is full of stately
    views,
Of borders, beds and shrubberies and lawns and
    avenues,
With statues on the terraces and peacocks strutting
    by;
But the Glory of the Garden lies in more than
    meets the eye.

For where the old thick laurels grow, along the
    thin red wall,
You'll find the tool- and potting-sheds which are
    the heart of all,
The cold-frames and the hot-houses, the dungpits
    and the tanks,
The rollers, carts and drain-pipes, with the barrows
    and the planks.

POEMS FROM HISTORY

And there you'll see the gardeners, the men and
    'prentice boys
Told off to do as they are bid and do it without
    noise;
For, except when seeds are planted and we shout
    to scare the birds,
The Glory of the Garden it abideth not in words.

And some can pot begonias and some can bud a
    rose,
And some are hardly fit to trust with anything
    that grows;
But they can roll and trim the lawns and sift the
    sand and loam,
For the Glory of the Garden occupieth all who come.

Our England is a garden, and such gardens are not
    made
By singing:—'Oh, how beautiful,' and sitting in the
    shade,

THE GLORY OF THE GARDEN

While better men than we go out and start their working lives
At grubbing weeds from gravel-paths with broken dinner-knives.

There's not a pair of legs so thin, there's not a head so thick,
There's not a hand so weak and white, nor yet a heart so sick,
But it can find some needful job that's crying to be done,
For the Glory of the Garden glorifieth every one.

Then seek your job with thankfulness and work till further orders,
If it's only netting strawberries or killing slugs on borders;
And when your back stops aching and your hands begin to harden,
You will find yourself a partner in the Glory of the Garden.

POEMS FROM HISTORY

Oh, Adam was a gardener, and God who made him sees
That half a proper gardener's work is done upon his knees,
So when your work is finished, you can wash your hands and pray
For the Glory of the Garden that it may not pass away!
And the Glory of the Garden it shall never pass away!

INDEX TO FIRST LINES

	PAGE
Across a world where all men grieve,	130
A. 'I was a "have."' B. 'I was a "have-not,"'	113
After the burial-parties leave,	56
Ah! What avails the classic bent,	80
A tinker out of Bedford,	33
At Runnymede, at Runnymede,	149
At two o'clock in the morning, if you open your window and listen,	152
Be well assured that on our side,	20
Brethren, how shall it fare with me,	29
Broke to every known mischance, lifted over all,	13
England's on the anvil—hear the hammers ring,	145
For all we have and are,	18
'Gay go up and gay go down,'	175
God rest you, peaceful gentlemen, let nothing you dismay,	37
'Have you news of my boy Jack?'	51
He passed in the very battle-smoke	27
I ate my fill of a whale that died,	101
I do not look for holy saints to guide me on my way,	96
If war were won by feasting,	164

INDEX TO FIRST LINES

	PAGE
If you stop to find out what your wages will be,	67
In a land that the sand overlays—the ways to her gates are untrod,	124
In the days of lace-ruffles, perukes and brocade,	167
It is always a temptation to an armed and agile nation,	143
Legate, I had the news last night. My cohort's ordered home,	137
'My son,' said the Norman Baron, 'I am dying, and you will be heir,'	146
Naked and grey the Cotswolds stand,	162
Not in the thick of the fight,	52
'Oh, where are you going to, all you Big Steamers,'	178
Oh ye who hold the written clue,	77
Once, after long-drawn revel at The Mermaid,	75
Once on a time was a King anxious to understand,	154
Our England is a garden that is full of stately views,	183
South and far south below the Line,	157
The Babe was laid in the Manger,	43
The banked oars fell an hundred strong,	3
The boats of Newhaven and Folkestone and Dover,	173
The dark eleventh hour,	9
The Doorkeepers of Zion,	25
The fans and the beltings they roar round me,	68
The first time that Peter denied his Lord,	104
The Garden called Gethsemane,	71
The overfaithful sword returns the user,	72

INDEX TO FIRST LINES

	PAGE
There are four good legs to my Father's Chair,	151
There are no leaders to lead us to honour, and yet without leaders we sally,	58
The road to En-dor is easy to tread,	46
These were never your true love's eyes,	100
The Sons of Mary seldom bother, for they have inherited that good part,	63
They shall not return to us, the resolute, the young,	54
'This is the State above the Law,'	88
Through learned and laborious years,	23
To-day, across our fathers' graves,	6
To the Judge of Right and Wrong,	31
Try as he will, no man breaks wholly loose,	94
'Twas not while England's sword unsheathed,	170
Twenty bridges from Tower to Kew,	135
'Twixt my house and thy house the pathway is broad,	36
We're not so old in the Army List	40
We thought we ranked above the chance of ill,	12
We were all one heart and one race,	7
We were taken from the ore-bed and the mine,	180
What boots it on the Gods to call?	48
'Whence comest thou, Gehazi,'	91
When Horse and Rider each can trust the other everywhere,	159
When Rome was rotten-ripe to her fall,	141
When the Himalayan peasant meets the he-bear in his pride,	107
Who in the Realm to-day lays down dear life for the sake of a land more dear?	83

www.ingramcontent.com/pod-product-compliance
Lightning Source LLC
LaVergne TN
LVHW030635080426
835510LV00022B/3373